The Woman's Book
of Courage

❀

Books by Sue Patton Thoele

The Courage To Be Yourself
The Courage To Be Yourself Journal
The Woman's Book of Confidence
Autumn of the Spring Chicken
Heart Centered Marriage

❀

The Woman's Book *of* Courage

....

MEDITATIONS FOR
EMPOWERMENT & PEACE
OF MIND

....

SUE PATTON THOELE

CONARI PRESS
Berkeley, CA

Conari Press books are distributed by Publishers
Group West

Cover design: Leigh Wells
Cover illustration: Rae Ecklund
Author photo: Paige Eden Thoele

ISBN: 1-57324-062-1

Library of Congress Cataloging-in-Publication Data

Thoele, Sue Patton
        The woman's book of courage : meditations for
    empowerment and peace of mind / Sue Patton
    Thoele–[Rev. ed.]
            p.   cm.
    ISBN 1-57324-062-1 (trade paper)
        1. Women Conduct of life. 2. Meditations.
        I. Title.
    [BJ1610.T46   1996]   96-33149
    158'.12–dc20   CIP

Printed in the United States of America on recycled paper

10 9 8 7 6 5 4

Acknowledgments

First I would like to thank Julie Bennett and Mary Jane Ryan, who, by believing in me and suggesting I write this book, gave me an opportunity to voice the things about which I feel the most passionate. Their professional expertise and personal friendship have enriched my life immeasurably. I would also like to thank my wonderful husband, Gene, and our equally wonderful kids for their unfailing support, kindness, enthusiasm, and hugs. I am so grateful to Joyce McKay, whose educated and loving feedback gave me the courage to vault my biggest emotional wall.

For the inspiration they have given me, I also wish to thank each of the writers whose words I have quoted. And a special thank-you to all the women whose stories I have shared in these pages. The courage you have shown in facing your fears and moving toward deeper personal and professional authenticity is an inspiration to me.

*To Annabelle Woodard, my
wisely courageous spiritual-mother
and mentor, from whom I first got the
inkling I might be courageous, too.*

Contents

. . . .

Introduction, xviii

I. **A Woman Has the Courage to Acknowledge Her Strength and Set Limits,** 2

Imagining Ourselves Strong, 4
Acting in Spite of Fear, 6
Knowing We Are Not the Target, 8
Chewing Bite-Size Pieces, 10
Putting Our White Horse out to Pasture, 12
Crediting Our Life's Account, 14
KISSING Our Life, 16
Saying "No" without Feeling Guilty, 18
Retiring Aunt Jemima, 20
Teaching Others How to Treat Us, 22

II. **A Woman Has the Courage to Love and Be Loved,** 24

Loving Our Inner Child, 26
Deserving Love, 28
Protecting Our Inner Child, 30
Asking to Be Nurtured, 32
Creating a Safe Place, 34
Filling Ourselves First, 36

Loving from Overflow, 38

Receiving from Others, 40

Forgiving for Our Own Good, 42

Forgiving Ourselves, 44

Adding a Dash of Kindness, 46

Loving Another's Inner Child, 48

III. **A Woman Has the Courage to Create Peace of Mind, 50**

Pausing in the Oasis of Silence, 52

Spending Our Moments Wisely, 54

Cleansing Our Emotional Bodies, 56

Creating Peace of Mind through Forgiveness, 58

Forgiving the Mother We Were, 60

Being Ourselves Today, 62

Resting in Unseen Arms, 64

Eliminating SHOULD, HAVE TO and CAN'T, 66

Imitating The Little Engine That Could, 68

Calming the Monkey-Mind, 70

Choosing "That's Good!", 72

Reprogramming Our Inner Mind, 74

Avoiding the Future Hole, 76

Keeping Afloat through Forgiveness, 78

Accepting the Unacceptable, 80

IV. **A Woman Has the Courage to Tame and Transform Her Dragons,** 82

Facing the Dragons of Fear, 84
Rejecting the Rejection Dragon, 86
Knowing We Can, 88
Sacking the Bag Lady, 90
Owning Our Own Excellence, 92
Refocusing Our Binoculars, 94
Healing through Feeling, 96
Rechoosing How We Want to Be, 98
Uprooting "Rootless" Fears, 100
Escaping the Depression Pit, 102
Chirping Up by Looking Up, 104
Feeling Worthwhile, 106

V. **A Woman Has the Courage to Be Her Own Good Friend,** 108

Disrobing the Inner Judge, 110
Tending Our Inner Garden, 112
Empowering Ourselves through Praise, 114
Accepting the Beauty of Our Imperfections, 116
Waking Up to Self-Love, 118
Receiving Validation, 120
Replenishing through Rest and Relaxation, 122

Discovering Our Personal Diamond, 124
Asking for What We Want and Need, 126

VI. **A Woman Has the Courage to Make Her Own Choices,** 128
Cruising with High-Altitude Attitudes, 130
Uncovering What We Want, 132
Growing Up Emotionally, 134
Inquiring Within, 136
Stopping Borrowed Trouble, 138
Daring to Risk, 140
Sidestepping Others' Negativity, 142
Selecting Positive People, 144

VII. **A Woman Has the Courage to Take Care of Her Body,** 146
Stimulating Our Natural Healing, 148
Encouraging Our Body, 150
Paying Attention to Our Body Wisdom, 152
Balancing and Harmonizing Ourselves, 154
Appreciating Our Bodies, 156
Being the Right Weight, 158
Aging as an Attitude, 160
Highlighting the Positives of Aging, 162
Oiling Our Apparatus Aerobically, 164

VIII. **A Woman Has the Courage to Communicate Lovingly,** 166

Pausing to Really Hear, 168

Listening Often Equals Loving, 170

Answering Silent Pleas, 172

Blowing Up, Not At, 174

Giving Roses without Thorns, 176

Agreeing on the Right Time, 178

Speaking Gently and Carrying a Soft Feather, 180

Kissing a Frog, 182

Honoring Ourselves by Speaking Out, 184

IX. **A Woman Has the Courage to Develope Healthy Relationships,** 186

Drying out the Responsibility Sponge, 188

Allowing Ourselves Limits, 190

Juggling the Balls of Motherhood, 192

Dragging Someone Else's Leg Irons, 194

Mothering, Not Smothering, 196

Breaking the Coffee-Fetching Cycle, 198

Enjoying Self-Confidence, 200

Becoming Friends with Our Lover, 202

Defanging Our Expectation Dragon, 204

X. **A Woman Has the Courage to Take Risks and Change,** 206

Becoming Response-able, 208

Unraveling Old Messages, 210

Releasing the Pain, Retaining the Memory, 212

Undergoing an Attitude Adjustment, 214

Exploring Our Shadows, 216

Leaving a Legacy of Authenticity, 218

Exposing Secrets to the Light, 220

Putting Superwoman out to Pasture, 222

XI. **A Woman Has the Courage to Recognize Rainbows,** 224

Recognizing Rainbows, 226

Opening to Miracles, 228

Focusing on Beauty, 230

Reaching through the Veil, 232

Seeing with the Eyes of Innocence, 234

Emulating Butterflies, 236

Laughing with Our Klutz, 238

Putting a Little Play in Our Day, 240

Detaching Compassionately through Play, 242

Nestling in the Arms of Nature, 244

XII. **A Woman Has the Courage to Claim the Goddess Within,** **246**

Training the Priestess in Us, 248

Accepting Our Credibility, 250

Dethroning the Virgin, 252

Tapping Invisible Power, 254

Making a difference, 256

Assimilating Both Saber and Scepter, 258

Serving as a Vessel, 260

Transforming and Transmuting
   Circumstances, 262

Gleaning Wisdom from Silence, 264

Transcending the Trojan Horse, 266

Adopting a Mentor-Mom, 268

Doing No Harm, 270

Personal Note, **272**

Author's Biography, **276**

Introduction

IN THE SIX YEARS SINCE I FIRST WROTE *The Woman's Book of Courage*, my unwavering faith in women's courage has been underscored countless times. I've been privileged to walk with women who are healing from excruciating losses and health challenges as well as those struggling through dark nights of the soul. And they have walked with me as I grappled with similar experiences. Together, holding hands and baring our hearts to one another, we have journeyed through the fires of hell to the mountaintops of light and joy.

No matter what the tribulation—whether it's negotiating a labyrinth of medical procedures or navigating through the darkness of disillusionment, despair, depression, the death of a loved one, or the need to regain our equilibrium after being marked by branding irons of shame or betrayal— women have incredible endurance and courage. It seems that even when seared by sorrow and shrouded in darkness, the vast majority of us eventually bob to the surface, bringing with us valuable insights and increased compassion for ourselves and others.

Each time I'm aware of myself or another woman bouncing back (sometimes it's a low, slow bounce) from a tremendous challenge, I become more deeply aware of how inherently courageous and wonderfully wise women are. Of course, if a person is addicted to chemicals or to the roles of victim and martyr, her capacity for courage and rejuvenation is severely curtailed. But, even then, there seems to be some inner nudging, saying, "Wake up! Life can be so much richer than this. You can feel, and be, so much more."

In addition to overcoming difficulties, women also have the courage to let daffodils bloom in their hearts, the wisdom to absorb the awesome joy of everyday miracles that surround us, and the ability to create cozy homes where love and laughter abound. Realistically, we're good! We're damn good! Unfortunately, we often don't truly believe that. Although we've made incredible strides toward equality, we're still prone to struggle with feelings of inadequacy and to shower our best—our compassion, our encouragement, our support—onto others while overlooking ourselves.

This is the area of our lives in which we need to increase our courage. It is essential that we expand our ability to treat ourselves with compassion, courtesy, and respect (even reverence). We need to have the boldness to remove the veil from our eyes and perceive ourselves as we genuinely are: beautiful, creative, loving beings with vast reservoirs of inner strength. Not without warts, of course; when we become aware of a wart sprouting, we can cultivate the courage to forgive ourselves and begin transforming the offending flaw. For most of us, forgiving our own imperfections and weaknesses is one of our hardest assignments. I know—it's definitely one of mine.

The Woman's Book of Courage is a compilation of meditations, affirmations, and true stories born out of my struggle to create my own feelings of emotional well-being and personal empowerment, instead of relying on other people or circumstances to give me a sense of strength and peace of mind. Like many women today, I often felt insecure and inadequate even though I appeared competent and successful. I longed to possess the characteristics others saw in me. Beginning a quest to have my inner feelings match my outer appearance, I soon discovered that the positive attitudes, beliefs, and feelings I longed for were shrouded in a fog of fear.

Courage is having the strength and willingness to overcome our resistance and do what we feel is right, even though it is difficult and/or we are afraid. It takes tremendous courage to face our fears, though it is essential that we do. For it is only when we free ourselves from the leg irons of fear, accepting and honoring the wisdom, strength, and beauty we inherently possess, that we can truly find the happiness we seek.

The Woman's Book of Courage evolved from my twenty years' experience as a psychotherapist. In those years, I learned many ways to help women in their search for empowerment and peace of mind. Now I want to share with you the affirmations and imagery that continue to stimulate courage in me, my friends, and my clients. The techniques in this book have become invaluable guides along our ever-evolving path toward self-realization.

I firmly believe that our triumphs and our failures, our joys and our sufferings are the result of our habitual thoughts—that what we believe in our innermost hearts will come true. Therefore, it is vitally important that we change the beliefs and expectations that keep us from experiencing success, peace of mind, and the ability to love fully.

What we have believed for many years often feels so true that it takes tremendous courage to have the strength to change those inner dictates. Affirmations and meditations are powerful tools for creative, positive change. Each segment in *The Woman's Book of Courage* gives you affirmations to use in reprogramming your subconscious. Many of the sections also provide a healing meditation in which you use your mind as a supportive friend.

When you first begin using affirmations, you may feel uncomfortable. That's okay. Allow time for your subconscious to absorb and accept a new belief, and have the courage and commitment to know that affirmations can heal on a deep level. As new beliefs begin to take hold in the fertile ground of your subconscious mind, your feelings will also change. It is not an immediate process, so be patient, because affirmations do work. Accompanied by vivid imagery, they work even faster.

The Woman's Book of Courage can be used in a number of ways—as a meditation guide, a daily reminder, or the answer to a specific question. You may want to open it at random, asking your higher self to guide you to the page that is right for you at this particular moment. Or you can use each of the twelve sections as a monthly study guide.

The affirmations and imagery in this book formed the basis of an ongoing women's group in which I took part for two years. It was a powerful experience for all of us. The group was a safe place where we learned to truly trust ourselves and each other. We found it much easier to have the courage to change, because we supported and were supported by others who had similar goals and desires. Sharing our frustrations and celebrating our progress fostered and facilitated our growth. Maybe you will want to form a group of your own, using the concepts in *The Woman's Book of Courage* as springboards for discussion.

I hope these meditations help you become aware of, acknowledge, and accept the courage you already possess and the courage you are growing into. They are meant to help you listen to yourself—for you, and only you, have your answers. We are all travelers on the often rocky path toward courageous and authentic living. We can create and maintain a positive, loving, and healthy attitude. We can increase peace of mind and feelings of empowerment. We can learn to listen to our intuition and claim the Goddess within.

A Woman Has the Courage To Acknowledge Her Strength and Set Limits

*Feminism called upon me to have the
courage to grow up, to discover and exercise
my womanly strength, to be unafraid of pain—
and the pain is immeasurable—knowing
that fully experienced, it makes
joy fully possible.*

—Sonia Johnson

OUR DAILY LIVES ARE PROOF OF OUR inherent strength. We women move through uncharted occupational territory, have and care for children, nurture others emotionally and physically, and explore our psychological and spiritual dimensions. Although we are usually strong for others, we often feel weak and victimized while attempting to set realistic limits that respect us as individuals. However, every human being has limits and, if we do not honor ours, we can become overextended, resentful, and even ill. So sometimes the most courageous thing we can do is be aware that we can t do it all for everyone.

Even when others disagree, it is important that we remember we have the right to be strong and to say no. When we know in our hearts that it is okay for us to honor ourselves by having limits, we can set them in a gentle way. Although it is one of the most difficult things women have to learn, often the courageous and loving thing for us to do is to acknowledge our strength and learn to set honest limits.

Imagining Ourselves Strong

WE ALL FACE SITUATIONS IN WHICH WE FEEL powerless and afraid. I once had a client who was terrified of an upcoming child custody hearing. She felt intimidated by the legal system, her lawyer, and especially her ex-husband. I asked her what it would take for her to feel safe and strong in the court room.

"Nothing short of riding in on a brahman bull!" she answered jokingly. It was a great idea, straight out of her inner wisdom.

I had her work with the image. She had fun creating the scenario of herself galloping into the court on a huge, snorting bull that threatened to gore anyone who tried to frighten her. Her day in court was a success because each time she felt the least bit scared she visualized herself astride her bull. With the help of her amusing but effective mental imagery she felt strong and capable. As a result, she was treated as if she were powerful, someone not to be dismissed or manipulated.

As the story illustrates, we are all as strong as we imagine ourselves to be. When we act as if we are strong, we move towards becoming the powerful women we desire to be.

Having the courage to see ourselves as strong, capable, and wise, able to do what we need and want helps make it so. But we need not do it alone. We can move creatively through our fears by accepting support and guidance from an unseen helper, whether that is a higher power or a brahman bull.

I am strong and capable.
I can do whatever I set my mind to.
I am filled with strength and confidence.

Acting in Spite of Fear

To act even though we are afraid is to be courageous. Amazingly, we do it almost every day. If we did not do what we feared, how many of us would move to a new state or decide to change jobs? More importantly, how many of us would be grappling with the intense need to be our own person if we were not, indeed, already courageous?

For years Fiona had felt at the mercy of her husband's temper. She was terrified by his outbursts; faced with his fury, she would appease him, suppressing her own feelings in the hopes he would calm down. Finally, cautiously she began to work on setting limits in her relationship. She talked to a therapist and went to Al-Anon meetings to help her have the courage to break the destructive pattern she was in with her husband. She knew she had succeeded when, on the eve of a trip to Hawaii, her husband blew up and said they were not going. Calmly, she continued to pack. With sadness but without anger, she told him she was sorry he felt as he did because she had been looking forward to a second honeymoon with him, but that she was going without him.

Getting to that point took tremendous courage for Fiona. She faced her fears and triumphed. Her story has a happy ending, too—her husband apologized for his outburst and they had a wonderful time in Hawaii.

Take a moment now to focus on your courageous acts. They can be very simple. If you are grieving, depressed, or otherwise in pain, it may take quite a bit of courage to do something as simple as getting out of bed or making dinner. Take a few moments to make a list of times when you have acted in spite of fear and then share your list with someone you trust. We are courageous every day, but it helps to remind us when we share our courage with others.

*I have the courage to act even though
I feel afraid.*

*I have the strength to do the things
I need to do.*

Knowing We Are Not the Target

WE OFTEN ALLOW OURSELVES TO BE DEEPLY wounded by the actions of people around us. We feel guilty and irrationally think that it is our fault if people treat us badly. It takes courage not to do this.

Sarah's father and sister were invariably doing and saying things that wounded her deeply She felt somehow responsible for their actions and became mired in guilt. One day, while visiting the zoo, she saw a gorilla bellowing and throwing excrement at onlookers. She realized that while she was among the crowd, she wasn't being personally targeted. Sarah decided to view the attacks of her father and sister in the same way. Now, when Sarah finds herself believing she is the target of her family's anger or manipulation, she pretends she is at the zoo observing another species and emotionally moves out of the line of fire.

It takes strength to know that we are not to blame for the actions of others, and that we do not need to be their target. Even if people insist on projecting their unfinished business onto us, we can train ourselves to remember that we are not responsible for what anyone else does or says. We can learn to take the bull's eye off our chest and put it in the closet.

I have the strength to know I am not the target.

*I know I don't need to "fix"
anyone else's attitude or circumstances.*

I dodge anger that is inappropriately aimed at me.

Chewing Bite-Size Pieces

. . . .

MANY TIMES OUR AUTOMATIC REACTION
when faced with an uncomfortable or confusing situation is to thrash around trying to
change it immediately. We attempt to swal-
low the whole predicament at once and spit it
out, solved. Very rarely does this approach
ease our pain or alter the situation. In fact,
thoughtless, quick action is often more frustrating than productive.

When baffled or upset, we need to PAUSE,
take a deep breath, and have the courage to
recognize that we are intelligent and resourceful enough to solve the problem. We
can either figure out a solution ourselves or
find the people to help us. Slowly and
thoughtfully, we can then begin to explore
the problem and its possible solutions in bite-
size pieces. Usually, as each small piece is
solved, anxiety subsides and the entire puzzle
fits together more easily than we might have
feared.

Who, for instance, hasn't experienced
qualms of inadequacy and frustration when
first faced with a convoluted income tax form
or an incomprehensible insurance form?

Without a small-step approach to such chores, we can feel discouraged before we even start. But if we pause, take a deep breath and affirm our ability to solve our problem, then divide our task into small pieces, we can almost always conquer whatever is in front of us.

We can find what we need to solve our problems if we don't allow ourselves to become overwhelmed. Three little slogans we can use to remind ourselves of this are: Pause, don't panic; this isn't an emergency; I rarely choke on bite-size pieces.

I am resourceful.

I take one thing at a time in bite-size pieces.

I solve problems with ease and intelligence.

Putting Our White Horse out to Pasture

....

WOMEN TEND TO BE HABITUAL RESCUERS. We leap on our white horses at the first sign of distress, believing that it is our job to save everyone. It isn't.

I was giving a talk at our local hospice meeting about how tiring it is to get stuck in the "rescue" mode. One woman volunteer exhaustedly said, "I agree, but what if your white horse is parked next to your husband's mule?" This woman had let herself be labelled The-One-Who-Fixes-It in her marriage, and her husband was stubbornly refusing to have it any other way. I asked her, "Do you believe you need to keep rescuing him?" Her answer was a hesitant, "Well, no, but. . . " Even though she was complaining, she really did believe it was her job. And of course, she couldn't get out of the position until she gave up her belief.

In reality, no one can rescue anyone else. Everyone must find his or her own way through life. However, breaking the white-horse habit is very difficult and takes commitment on our part. We need to keep reminding ourselves that, although society has fostered the myth of woman-as-rescuer, it is invalid. As we have the courage to continually halt our white horse in mid-gallop we will, in time, believe it is okay to do so.

I know I can rescue only myself.

I put my white horse out to pasture.

I trust others know how best to live their lives.

Crediting Our Life's Account

THE MYRIAD OF DEMANDS ON OUR TIME and energy can leave us feeling emotionally drained and physically exhausted. We become imbalanced when we give out more than we take in. Because women have been taught to be givers and receiving seems selfish to us, it takes enormous courage to see the value in allowing ourselves to give only that which is reasonable and healthy.

If your life were a bank account, how many daily deposits and withdrawals do you make to and from the account of your body, feelings, mind, and spirit? In fact, we all do have a "life account," from which we frequently make too many withdrawals or allow others to withdraw too freely.

In order to have a comfortable "balance" in our lives, we need to credit liberally and debit wisely. When we overdraw physically, emotionally, mentally, or spiritually, we "see red"; i.e., we experience frustration, anger, and exhaustion. But when we credit our life's account by setting realistic limits, we have more to give. Although taking care of ourselves is often difficult to do, it is an excellent investment in creating the quality of life we want and deserve. By taking the time to nurture ourselves, we ensure that we will not get "overdrawn."

I credit my "life account"
by setting realistic limits.

I have the courage to decide
what I will give and what I will not give.

My life is blessed
by balance and harmony.

KISSING Our Life

. . . .

"YES" IS A LITTLE WORD, BUT IT CAN LEAD
to lots of complications in our lives if we use
it too liberally. Saying "No" is particularly
hard for women because we feel guilty turning down requests or demands. We want to
live up to our own and others' expectations,
even if they are unreasonable.

How often do you find yourself overwhelmed by more commitments than you can
comfortably handle, wondering, "Why did I
say 'Yes' to this commitment? I knew I didn't
really want to do it." One of the biggest reasons we say "Yes" is because we don't honor
our limits—many of us aren't even aware of
them until it's too late. But we all need to give
ourselves permission to be aware of our limits,
to listen to the inner warnings as they come,
and then honor our wisdom by saying "No."

One way to begin to do this is to imple-
ment the old KISS philosophy of Keep It
Simple, Sweetie. Say "No" to complexity and
"Yes" to simplicity in your life. Complexity is
exhausting and fragmenting while simplicity
is energizing and centering.

Write a list of ways you can simplify your

life. What obligations can you delegate to others, give up altogether, or modify in order to be comfortable with your commitments and feel you have not overstepped your limits? Gently close your eyes and visualize yourself living more simply. Having weeded out unnecessary responsibilities and commitments from your schedule, think of things you find nourishing, such as solitude, friendship, or romance, and visualize yourself enjoying them. We deserve to have a simply beautiful life.

I am aware of my limits and I honor them.

I give myself permission to keep my life simple.

I create the time to do things which nourish me.

Saying "No"
without Feeling Guilty

....

WHAT IN THE WORLD IMPELS US TO SAY "Yes" when we feel "No"? We think we should. We're afraid of what they will think of us if we don't do what they want.

Vickie tearfully lamented to me, "I knew it wouldn't work when Jack (her husband) asked if he could come to work for me. Now he's there and I hate it! Why did I say "Yes?" Vickie had been taught to feel guilty if she refused a request. She is not alone—we women have been brainwashed to ignore what we feel is right for us if it doesn't comply with what others want. That's why it takes a lot of courage to stand up for ourselves and set limits; if we don't we can end up filled with regret and resentment, as Vickie did.

Even though we are afraid of disappointing others, when we really feel we have a right to say "No" and say it with full awareness of that right, people usually think it's just fine. For when we expect people to accept our No's and to honor our limits, they generally do. Our conviction that we have the right to choose to say "No" comes across and is accepted.

So we need to respectfully pay attention to ourselves, tuning in when the little voice inside wants to say "No." We are our own best experts. We can replace our draining shoulds with empowering words like can, want to, choose to, or will.

I have the right to say "No" without feeling guilty.

I have the courage to say "No" without feeling guilty.

I pay attention to what I know is right for me.

Retiring Aunt Jemima

LURKING IN THE SUBCONSCIOUS OF SOME women is the archaic belief that as a woman, wife, and mother, our proper role is willing servant to our families. Mindy came face to face with her hidden belief about the role she felt she played when she saw her family's Christmas photo. The idea had been for each family member to dress in outfits that indicated one of their main interests. The children were dressed in sports uniforms or theatrical costumes, and her husband wore his jogging togs. Mindy had chosen Aunt Jemima. She thought she dressed as a slave for a joke, but, after seeing the picture and thinking about her reasons for choosing as she did, she became aware that she really did feel like a slave. And she began to comprehend how resentful she felt as a result.

Realizing the role she had allowed herself to slip into was a turning point in her life. She decided to send Aunt Jemima into retirement. She began affirming that she deserved to be her own person. As that belief took hold, she was able to set firm limits about how much she would do for everyone and stick with them. She also began seriously to pursue her career. It wasn't easy, but the eventual bonus for Mindy and her family was that she began to feel more loving and giving as she gave up her slave role and became committed to having a life of her own.

It takes courage to retire Aunt Jemima and give ourselves permission to do what we choose to do rather than what we feel we have to do. As we gather the strength to give up living under the tyranny of our shoulds, we will feel more loving, and our giving will not be laced with resentment. We have the right to set limits and have lives of our own.

*I have the right to set limits
and the courage to do so.*

*Setting reasonable limits
makes me more loving to myself and my family.*

Teaching Others
How to Treat Us

A BURDENSOME PROBLEM MANY OF US HAVE is the inability to accept our own worth. At some deep level we believe that we are not worthy of success, happiness, or supportive and loving relationships.

There is an old adage that "we teach people how to treat us." Do you teach those around you to treat you with respect or disrespect? When we believe we are unworthy, others treat us accordingly, but when we believe we are worthy of being treated well, we will accept nothing less. Inherently, we are worthy—our challenge is to know that and treat ourselves as we want others to treat us.

Recently a dear friend of mine discovered that for years she had been silently screaming at men, "How dare you treat me the way I feel about myself!" Now that she loves and accepts herself, others (even men) do, too.

You too can feel worthy of good treatment. Quietly close your eyes and recreate a time when you felt valued and accepted by yourself and others. If you can't think of an actual incident, make one up. Allow yourself to soak up the wonderful feeling of being treated well and with respect. Assure yourself that you deserve this excellent treatment. Let the feeling seep in to the very cells of your body. Revel in it.

Then, holding that mantle of good feeling around and through you, imagine a time when you were ill-treated. From a sense of deserving to be treated well, change the uncomfortable scene. Insist on acceptable behavior toward you. If the people in your visualization are not willing to treat you acceptably, walk away from the situation. Remove yourself. We all deserve to be treated well.

I deserve to be treated well.

I accept only acceptable behavior toward me.

I have the courage to teach people to treat me well.

A Woman Has
the Courage to Love
and Be Loved

*As selfishness and complaint pervert
and cloud the mind, so love with its joy
clears and sharpens the vision.*

—Helen Keller

NOTHING TAKES MORE COURAGE than to open ourselves to the risks inherent in loving. To love is to be available and accessible to another—physically, emotionally, mentally, and spiritually. And, when we do that, aren't we vulnerable to the pain involved? If we have experienced ugly or hurtful circumstances, such as incest or emotional abandonment, under the guise of love, we are especially wary of love.

Loving (at least, giving to and caring for) others is one of the things women have had the courage to do best. But have we been able to love ourselves or allow others to love us? Feeling lovable springs from a healed inner child who feels she is worthy of love. Many of these pages will deal with nurturing the wounded little girl inside ourselves, so we can give and accept love in healthy ways.

As we have the courage to heal our past by looking back and inward—an often painful process—we can find ways to love ourselves and to truly love others. It is our right and responsibility, as well as our joy, to love and be loved.

Loving Our Inner Child

AT LEAST ONE ACTOR IN OUR INNER CAST of characters is a wounded child who is at times shy, frightened, or in pain. She doesn't feel courageous or brave. Life seems awfully scary to her. Gently befriending our inner little girl and helping her feel safe in the world is taking a giant step toward emotional freedom and inner courage. For a healed child within creates an adult able to love and be loved.

It is often valuable to acknowledge our inner child with a comforting gift such as a teddy bear. Leigh has a soft, hand-sized teddy bear. At first she felt silly and embarrassed to admit that she, an intelligent grown woman, sometimes, during stressful periods in her life, wanted to hold her bear as she fell asleep. When she had the courage to allow her little girl the comfort she sought, she realized her bear symbolized "mother" to her since it had graced the bed of her own mother as she struggled with her final illness.

Take a few minutes and close your eyes. Imagine yourself in a beautiful setting where you feel comfortable and safe. Invite your little girl to join you. She may appear as a photograph you remember of yourself as a child, a symbolic representation of you, or you may only sense her presence. Anything you see is right. She may not trust you at first, so be gentle and take your time getting to know her. Talk to her, sit with her, listen to her, hold her. In the warmth of your love, acceptance, and attention, she will heal.

I have the courage to see my inner child as lovable.

My inner child is acceptable to me and to others.

I unconditionally love and accept my inner little girl.

Deserving Love

. . . .

UNTIL WE REALLY BELIEVE WE DESERVE to be loved, chances are we will not draw healthy loving to us. Maybe, as a child, we were told we were bad; or maybe we assumed we were unacceptable from the treatment we received. Until about the age of seven, children feel everything that happens to them, or even around them, is their fault. As adults we rationally know that we were not unlovable as children, and that our parents and other important adults did the best they could considering their own wounds and limitations. But knowing we are lovable needs to register in our hearts as well as our minds.

Alice, well loved by her friends and family, always had the nagging feeling that someday everyone would realize they were mistaken about her and leave. She uncovered the reason for her feeling during a visualization when she vividly remembered a nun having her, for some minor infraction, fill a notebook page with, "I, Alice, am a bad girl." To help heal the label of "bad" which had plagued her all her life, Alice brought into her visualization a warm and kind mother figure who erased the original sentence and encouraged Alice to write, "I, Alice, am a good girl."

Because the concept of deserving love can be one of our most vulnerable areas—the home of some of our deepest fears—it takes a great deal of courage to look at our feelings of lovability. Therefore, we need to notice when we hear ourselves saying, "Oh well, maybe I don't deserve love," and become a loving and reassuring mother to our inner child, the kind of mother we all dreamed of having, always affectionate, available, and accepting. It is never too late to have a happy childhood. We can become loving parents to ourselves.

I am lovable.
I deserve to be loved.

Protecting Our Inner Child

MANY OF OUR ARGUMENTS, DISAGREE-
ments, and other painful encounters actually
are between the wounded children inside
each of us and not between the adults we appear to be. Once, when my partner and I
were explaining the concept of inner children
at a seminar, a woman participant began furi-
ously waving at us for attention. She exclaimed, "You just saved my marriage! I don't
hate all of my husband, I just hate and fear his
mean inner little boy!"

When children are being unreasonable we
create a "time-out" to allow them to vent their
feelings alone. We can do this as adults too.
Mary Beth, a client of mine, said, "It really
hurts me when I have to listen to my husband
tell me how stupid I am." She didn't have to;
in fact it would have been better if she didn't.
I encouraged her to recognize his little boy
was having a temper tantrum when he berated
her, and to leave the room until he cooled
down and could talk on an adult level. Staying
in the same room and allowing his inner little
boy to harangue her hooked her wounded little
girl and then the fur really flew between them.

If we find ourselves in a childish and destructive disagreement, we need to protect our own and the other person's inner child by venting away from each other and returning to the confrontation as adults. Conflict between wounded inner children never leads to a better understanding of one another or helps a relationship improve.

I love and respect my inner child.
I keep my inner child safe and protected.
I vent my feelings in a positive and loving way.

Asking to Be Nurtured

No matter how old or mature we are, there are times when we need to be nurtured as if we were a child. Six months after my mother's death, I was frustrated and worried by some snags in the publishing of my first book. In order to meet a crucial deadline, I needed to call the typesetter. I was nine digits into the telephone number when I realized I was calling my mother's number. Crying and trembling, I understood my inner child was in despair and said to my husband, "I'm about four years old right now and I need my mommy. Would you please hold me?" He did, and my little girl sobbed out her frustration and grief.

When our inner child reaches out and asks for solace we must find someone who can respond lovingly. We need to be clear it is our inner child who needs the support. It was easier for my husband to hold and comfort a sobbing four year old than it would have been for him to console a near-hysterical adult. We know how to nurture kids, and we are not as afraid of their feelings as we might be of adults'.

Just because we live in an adult body doesn't mean we don't experience childlike feelings. Having the courage to ask for the nurturing we need helps us move through our feelings more quickly and effectively.

*I recognize my inner child's need
to reach out for comfort.*

*I give myself permission
to ask for comfort and solace.*

I love my needy inner child.

Creating a Safe Place

....

WE ALL NEED A REFUGE, A SAFE HARBOR IN which to rest and be replenished—a sanctuary created by the magical mystery of our imagination. Such a haven might be a beautiful green, sheltered garden where we meet, talk with, and are comforted by a wise and loving advisor. In our often fragmented days it is important for us to create such a sanctuary, a place from which to gather the courage, strength, and balance to creatively live our daily lives. An inner garden is often the most powerful solace we can find.

Close your eyes now and imagine yourself in a beautiful place. Feel yourself wrapped in the healing and protective embrace of someone who has only your best interest at heart. If no one you know comes to mind, create a loving person. Rest in her or his arms—a precious and valued child protected from all harm. Feel the caring, and carry the feeling throughout your day.

After we have established an inner retreat, we can return to it by merely remembering its beauty and peace. If there is a time in our day when we need reassurance or peace of mind, we can take a moment or two to revisit our sanctuary and be replenished in the safe embrace of our inner guardian.

I am loved and protected.

I am safe in the world.

*I use my wise imagination
to create a safe harbor for myself.*

Filling Ourselves First

WE KNOW IT IS IMPORTANT FOR OUR sense of well-being to give. In fact, there has been a scientific study which shows that the immune system responds positively when we help others and can be activated by merely watching a film about someone helping others.

But it is not healthy to give until we feel drained, used, and deprived. Such giving can be laced with hostility, resentment, anger, and the unspoken message: "Now you owe me!" This is not loving; this is bartering. We love best from a sense of overflow. When we are brimming with the energy that comes with having the courage to take care of ourselves first, our love and caring are freely given gifts, with nothing expected in return.

Our minds may tell us that filling ourselves first is an act of selfishness—it seems to go against society's dictum, particularly addressed to women, that it is more blessed to give than receive. It takes a tremendous amount of courage to realize that filling ourselves is essential. It takes even more courage to know how to do it, especially if we are out of the habit of thinking about nourishing ourselves.

To help move into the healthy pattern of filling yourself, ask yourself these questions and jot down the answers: What replenishes me so that I can love freely? What small step can I take today to allow time for myself to fill and refill?

We can do ourselves, and those we love, a favor by having the courage to fill our life's vase; by making a commitment to ourselves that, in order to be a free-flowing, clear fountain of love, we will fill ourselves first.

I give myself permission
to fill my vase to overflowing.

I freely love others from a sense of overflow.

It is loving for me to fill my own vase.

Loving from Overflow

BECAUSE TAKING TIME FOR OURSELVES IS often a foreign idea, we need to have helpful reminders. When Verna turned fifty-nine, she decided it was time she had an adolescence. As the eldest daughter of an old-fashioned German family, she had been the designated mother's helper and servant. Leaving her parents' home, she married and had six children of her own. Circumstances such as illness, moves, and the usual responsibilities of a large family dictated that she put herself last.

Never thinking of herself was such an ingrained habit that even now, at age seventy-eight, she needs to give herself reminders to do so, such as paying her tuition in advance when she returned to school recently.

Many of us are in the same boat as Verna. We want to lighten our lives and nurture ourselves, but we don't know how. It helps to make a list of what fills us, gives us joy, and feels nurturing and healing. We need to check how much these people, activities, places, and attitudes we've listed are a part of our lives.

In order to absorb the feeling of receiving,

sit quietly and close your eyes. Gently ask for the picture of a vase, which represents you, your life's vessel, to come into your mind's eye. If the picture you see is not one you like, change it until you have a vase that pleases you. Now visualize all of the fulfilling things you listed pouring into your vase. If good things refuse to fill your vase, stop and write in a journal any reasons you may feel unworthy. Gently, gently reassure yourself that you deserve to have what you want and need. And, remember, we love others best from our own overflow.

I open myself to receive all good things.

*I love others unconditionally
from the fullness of my own heart.*

Receiving from Others

. . . .

LAURA, A YOUNG, BEAUTIFUL, AND BRAVE woman I knew, recently died. For months before her death, women from her church volunteered their time working in her dress shop when she was too ill to be there. During that time Laura shared with them her feelings that her life had been good, and one of the best things about it was being able to fulfill her dream of having her own shop. In helping Laura, her friends gave her the gift of a dream realized, and she gave them the gift of feeling useful.

It is often tough for women to do, but there are times when it is healthy for us to allow others to nurture and care for us. Our lives are so much about serving others, being busy and useful, that we forget the value in balancing giving and receiving.

When we are sad, confused, depressed, or ill, it is important for us to allow ourselves to reach out and ask for what we want and need, even though to do so is scary. We will give those who care about us the precious gift of being able to help us, and give ourselves the gift of being supported when we need it. It is much easier for us to move through our feelings when we let go of the isolating belief that we should "go it alone." We need and deserve support.

I allow others to support me.
I deserve to be loved and supported.
*I have the courage to ask
for help and emotional support.*

Forgiving for Our Own Good

WE ALL HAVE PEOPLE IN OUR LIVES WE need to forgive—for our own good. None of us has gone through life without feeling hurt in some way or another. But to harbor resentment is to clog up our own flow of love and good feelings.

Forgiveness originally meant to "return good treatment for ill usage." Pamela discovered the importance of forgiveness when her husband left her for her best friend. Needless to say, she felt ill-used by them both. For a while she let feelings of hate and betrayal eat away at her, which caused her a great deal of mental anguish and didn't hurt either one of them a bit. As she had the courage to begin forgiving—first herself for her part in the marriage failure, and then her husband and friend—her whole life began to flow more freely. Her hurt and lack of forgiveness had blinded her to the love and support she did have from her children, family, and friends. As she forgave, Pamela was able to begin healing.

Lack of forgiveness clouds our ability to see the beauty in our lives and destroys our peace of mind. Carrying around hurt, disappointment, and resentment over the times we felt ill-used is like wearing several overcoats in Hawaii: hot, heavy, and hindering. Forgiving allows us to emotionally dress so that we can enjoy the balmy breezes.

Forgiveness is a process, and we need to allow ourselves to take one little step at a time. Our first courageous step is to be willing to give up our hurt—which often is terribly difficult—and focus on having a true willingness to forgive. If we only pretend we've forgiven someone because we know we should, it's like candying a rotten apple—it may look good on the outside but it's still rotten on the inside. We can activate our willingness to forgive and eventually actually be forgiving.

I am willing to be willing to forgive_____.

I am willing to forgive_____.

I forgive_____ .

Forgiving Ourselves

WE ARE ALL PERFECTLY HUMAN AND, therefore, do or feel things we need to forgive ourselves for. Michelle, a young woman I worked with, had been in a long-term, destructive, addictive love affair. She ended that relationship but, as time went on, felt progressively worse about herself and didn't have the courage to sustain another relationship even though several young men had been interested in her. She was miserable, paralyzed by confusion and self-doubt. One day I asked her, "What would it be like for you if you forgave yourself for your relationship with Kevin?" She looked at me in total surprise and then broke into tears. Until that moment, it had never occurred to her even to consider forgiving herself for the mistake of choosing Kevin.

Unfortunately, Michelle's story is not that unique. Many of us strive to adopt the Golden Rule toward others but often forget to apply it to ourselves. We do unto ourselves as we would never dream of doing unto others.

Although we have been encouraged to forgive others, statements such as, "Aren't you ashamed of yourself?" have given us the belief that self-shame is fine but forgiving oneself is taboo. However, self-forgiveness is vital. Only in an atmosphere of forgiveness can we have the courage to be who we really are. When we do not forgive ourselves for our mistakes, we encase ourselves in an emotional straitjacket, afraid to risk, create, or feel.

We can start the forgiving process by making a list of what we want to forgive ourselves for. Choose one thing and for a week, insert it in the affirmation below. Then go through the rest of your list in the same way. Forgiving ourselves makes us more open to loving others.

I love and forgive myself as I would a dear friend.
I, totally and without reservation, forgive myself
for_____.

Adding a Dash of Kindness

BECAUSE WE MAY SUSPECT THAT "NICE gals finish last," it can be hard for us to open our hearts fully to others for fear of being hurt. It takes courage to add a dash of kindness to all of our encounters, especially if we have been wounded in the past. But if we can remember that nice wears well, and that our actions tend to draw similar reactions, it might be easier for us to believe being kind is safe.

We always have a choice about how to act, and when we choose to add a dash of kindness to our attitudes and actions, we bring joy and comfort not only to those on the receiving end but to ourselves as well. Giving a smile and a kind word usually elicits a similar response, and certainly lightens and brightens any encounter.

Authentic kindness (as opposed to play-acting "nice" because we are motivated by fear or guilt), a from-the-heart desire to reach out in love and compassion, is a reflection of who we really are—beings of love. Choosing to think, speak, and act with love—from the very center of ourselves—creates an ever-widening circle of love, kindness, and respect in our family, city, the world.

At times it may take every bit of courage we can muster to do so, but choosing to add a dash of kindness to our everyday activities is choosing to live in an attitude of love. As women, our highest calling is to extend and expand love. The best place to begin is with ourselves in our personal lives.

I express myself with love and kindness.
I have the courage to be nice, and I enjoy it.
I communicate who I really am—a being of love.

Loving Another's Inner Child

. . . .

THERE ARE TIMES WHEN ANOTHER PERSON'S inner child treats us badly. It's very tempting to react from our own inner child and either become defensive or feel victimized. Since courage is partly having the willingness to do what we know is right even though it is difficult, it is courageous to choose to act lovingly when faced with someone's petulant inner child.

Penny's adult son was going through a period of blaming her for his unhappiness. After their initial conversation concerning his feelings about her failures as a mother, she was a wreck—alternately enraged and grief-stricken. She didn't sleep all night and the entire roof of her mouth became one big canker sore. Then she began to comfort and console her inner child, who was so ready to take the blame for her son's life, by reminding herself of all the good things she had said and done. With continual reassurance that she had done the best she could, she was eventually able to respond appropriately to her son's inner little boy.

When faced with raw, childish feelings in

other people we are often tempted to say, "Oh, grow up!" But we need to look behind the outward behavior and know that their inner children are crying out. With that awareness we have a greater capacity to nurture the child inside.

If other people do not allow us to nurture them, we can at least feel compassion for their hurting child, rather than intimidated or guilt-ridden by their facades. It is easier to do this if, in our mind's eye, we see the adult we are dealing with as a two year old. Imagining an appealing baby in distress will help keep us from feeling intimidated and, therefore, allow us to feel safe enough to love.

*I love, nurture, and respect
the inner child I see in others.*

I listen to the inner child in myself and others.

A Woman Has
the Courage to Create
Peace of Mind

"Where you tend a rose, my lad,
A thistle cannot grow."

—Frances Hodgson Burnett

MUCH OF OUR DAILY LIFE SEEMS in direct opposition to acquiring peace of mind. We are often busy, rushed, and over-committed, which keeps us out of balance and off center. Because the world seems to live without peace of mind— addicted to chaos, chemicals, and calamity— it is courageous for us to take a different path and say, "This is not for me."

Committing to moving toward peace of mind, no matter what the circumstance, is a constant struggle for many of us. In fact, we often believe that mental turmoil is the norm and serenity an unrealistic Pollyanna dream, but that is not true. Peace of mind is attainable. Serenity is possible. We can have them both; not always, but a good majority of the time. Having the courage and strength to insert quiet time into our schedules and change disturbing thought patterns and beliefs to life-affirming ones is a gift we have the power to give ourselves.

Pausing in the Oasis of Silence

WITH OUR FAST-LANE EXISTENCE IT IS easy to neglect quiet time, to feel there are more important things to do. But it is in the quiet that we are replenished, renewed, and recharged for the demands of our lives. In silence we can reconnect with our true source of energy and inner wisdom. The "still, small voice" is heard more in the silence beyond, around, and beneath language than it is in the cacophony of incessant sound.

As much as our physical body needs water in order to live, we need silence in order to have a rich emotional and spiritual life. To illustrate the importance of silence to the soul, we can recall a time when we were very thirsty and longed for the relief of a cool drink of water. In the same way, our souls yearn for the refreshing relief of silence.

Because lives focused on outward activity rather than inner contemplation seem more socially acceptable, it takes courage to have the self-discipline to pause each day in the oasis of silence. However, it is important that we persevere—for in quiet solitude, listening only to the sounds of ourselves, we can begin to hear the whispers and urgings of our own inner guidance.

Only in the oasis of silence can we drink deeply from our inner cup of wisdom.

I find peace and serenity in silence.

I take time to be silent.

I listen to and trust my inner wisdom.

Spending Our Moments Wisely

DO WE LIVE IN THE PRESENT OR, AS Hugh Prather says, "rehearse difficulties to come"? It's far too easy for many of us to fall into the trap of worrying about what may happen in the future or lamenting what happened in the past—neither of which do we have control over now.

Suppose someone gave us $1440 each day for the rest of our lives, but we had to spend all $1440 that day; none of it could be taken into the next. Each of us has been given something more priceless than dollars, 1440 minutes every day. Do we get our money's worth?

Living in the moment sounds good, but how do we learn to do it? Awareness is the key. We need to be aware of where our thoughts are, which means we need to have the strength to live consciously. When we discover our thoughts wandering back to the unchangeable past or forward into the unforeseeable future, we can choose to bring our awareness back to now, this moment.

Now is the only moment we truly have to live. Yesterday is irretrievable and tomorrow is unknown. Living in the moment is having the courage to live consciously, with awareness.

I have the courage to live in the moment.

I savor each minute given me.

I appreciate each priceless day I live.

Cleansing Our
Emotional Bodies

JUST AS WE WASH OUR BODIES AND OUR clothes, we need to cleanse our emotional bodies. As we move through our days, many of us act as psychic garbage collectors vacuuming in other people's feelings. Women are especially prone to taking on everyone else's problems. The more sensitive we are, the more debris we collect. Since we have more than enough of our own baggage to deal with, it is essential we have the courage to let go of that which is not ours to carry. Cleansing our emotional bodies gives us the stamina and energy to begin another day.

In order to free ourselves from inappropriate feelings we have been subjected to during the day, it is wise to experientially symbolize purifying our emotional bodies.

One excellent way to do this is to take a shower or bath and, as you soak in or stand under the pouring water, imagine any limiting, defeating, and depressing feelings or beliefs being rinsed away. In as vivid a way as you can, see the emotions that are not yours swirling down the drain away from you. It is not your responsibility to shoulder them. Now visualize and feel the purifying water saturating the cleansed areas with love and energy.

I let go of feelings that are not mine.

I am fresh and clean.

I am full of love and energy.

Creating Peace of Mind
through Forgiveness

IT IS DIFFICULT TO CREATE A FLOW OF
forgiveness toward people with whom we are
angry or who we feel have wronged us. People whom we have not forgiven have power
over us—our thoughts and our moods. When
we forgive, we free ourselves to have greater
peace of mind.

At work Lillian supervised a woman whose
main goals in life seemed to be irritating her
co-workers and getting out of doing her share
of the work. The fact that bureaucratic loop-
holes made it impossible for the woman to be
fired caused Lillian to arrive at the office each
day a little more tense than the day before.

She found the following exercise very
helpful in encouraging her heart to open,
thereby diluting the power she had allowed
the woman to have over her emotions. We all
probably have someone in our lives we could
try it on.

Close your eyes and picture a person or
thing you love unconditionally. Your picture
may be a flower, a child, or a place—whatever

or whoever gives you the feeling of a full heart. See your heart overflowing toward the loved object. Feel the flow of energy toward the beloved. Take time to enjoy feeling the expansion of your heart. Now, very gently, allow your original picture to fade and in its place bring the image of the troublesome person. Keep the loving flow going toward the new image. If you find it impossible to continue the flow, that's okay, just try it again at a later time. Eventually, you will be able to allow love to flow.

You do not need to feel affectionate toward the person, but in order to experience peace of mind, you do need to love him or her impersonally. Loving impersonally means you wish him or her well or, at least, wish them no harm.

Each day I am more and more able to love and forgive.

I allow love to flow through me to_____.

I forgive_____.

Forgiving the Mother
We Were

WE ARE SO VULNERABLE ABOUT OUR MOTHering abilities. It's all too easy for us to feel guilty. Have we done too much or not done enough? Are we too strict or too permissive? Questions such as these can haunt us whether our children are fourteen days old or fortyseven years old. But in order to have peace of mind, we need to forgive the mother we were. This takes great courage, particularly in the face of society's attitude of "it-must-bemother's-fault," no matter what "it" is.

When my first child was born, I was young, inexperienced, and unhappy—and not too great a mother. I wanted to be good, I tried to be good, but I wasn't the kind of good mother I eventually became.

Before I could relax and be the mother I wanted to be, I needed to forgive the struggling young mother I was originally. I did that by picturing myself in my early twenties, acknowledging my loneliness and confusion, and then assuring myself that I did the best I could at the time. And I had.

If you need to forgive the mother you were, allow yourself to close your eyes and

...knowing that helps us to forgive ourselves and, in a climate of forgiveness, we can become better than we were. If our relationships with our children are secure enough, after we heal our shame at not being a perfect parent, we may eventually want to talk to them about our regrets and ask for their forgiveness.

I forgive myself for my past mothering.

I am the best mother I can be.

I lovingly support all children in my care.

Being Ourselves Today

AS WE COURAGEOUSLY WORK TO BECOME truly ourselves, each new day presents us with opportunities to unfold in the perfectly right way. A very wise woman once told me that "the future depends on a healed past and a well-lived present."

We create a fulfilling future, and honor our present, by living this day in a manner that will enable us to look back tomorrow with pride. Each day we can learn, from whatever sources inspire us, to love ourselves just as we are—unfinished and still struggling—and to live with our families, co-workers, and friends as a kind and considerate equal.

The talents, abilities, and idiosyncrasies we bring to this life are uniquely ours, and we are invited to share them with others in our own special way.

At the top of a sheet of paper write the heading, What Makes Me Unique? Then, writing as if you were your best friend, jot down several of your special attributes. For fun you might want to add a few quirks also.

We are one of a kind. Our individuality is a precious gift—a gift too sacred to be thrown away. It is our right, privilege, and responsibility to be ourselves today.

Today, I have the courage to be uniquely myself.

*I give thanks for the gifts
that I, alone, have to share.*

*I accept the past, enjoy the present,
and look forward to the future.*

Resting in Unseen Arms

So much of our anxiety and insecurity comes from the deep fear that we are alone, adrift without guidance. It isn't so. We are uplifted and supported by many unseen, but present, friends and mentors.

One day during my mother's struggle with cancer, I was overcome with the frustration of living 1500 miles away, discouraged by our family's interactions, and bereft at the thought of losing her. At the point of collapse, I picked up a favorite little book, *The Quiet Mind*, and turned to a page at random. I read, "We know, Dear Child, how hard life can be, but we are ever with you." Seeing that sentence, I relaxed in to a cleansing torrent of tears and had the most comforting feeling of being held. I didn't just think it, I truly felt nestled in the arms of someone who cared.

It was the words "Dear Child" that spoke to me since it was my inner little girl, soon to be motherless, who was inconsolable. My adult self, about to lose a friend, was not able to comfort the inner child as well as usual, so the thought and the feel of outside arms, ever near, was a balm.

Remembering to pause and ask for consolation, when we are in need, brings us calming peace of mind. Imagining ourselves in the loving embrace of someone who unconditionally cares for us soothes and quiets our quaking inner child.

I allow myself to rest in the unseen arms of God.

*I am supported and loved
by unseen friends and mentors.*

I have the courage to accept comfort.

Eliminating SHOULD, HAVE TO *and* CAN'T

ONE OF THE GREATEST HINDRANCES TO peace of mind is the way we talk to ourselves in the privacy of our own minds. As a therapist, I see many people who have a judgmental, parental voice inside that says, "You can't do it right. You didn't do enough. You should have known! You're wrong...you're bad." How would our house plants react if we talked to them the way we talk to ourselves? Would they wither or thrive? Would our friends trust and confide in us, if we spoke to them the way we speak to ourselves?

Unfriendly self-talk causes great stress. We can eliminate at least thirty-five percent of our stress immediately by erasing the words SHOULD, HAVE TO, and CAN'T from our vocabulary. SHOULD, HAVE TO and CAN'T are victim words. They imply we have no power, no choice. We can empower ourselves by replacing these victim words with CHOOSE TO, WANT TO, and WILL.

Because we have believed there are certain things we have to do, even more things we should do, and many things we can't do, it is very difficult to acknowledge that what our minds are telling us is not necessarily true. We simply don't have to, but we certainly may choose to do, think, or feel something.

Creating empowering self-talk is very simple—although not easy—and we're totally in charge of doing it. It starts with acknowledging that we have the power to decide to speak to ourselves in a positive way and then committing to do so.

I speak to myself in a loving manner.

*I use empowering words
such as choose to, want to, and will.*

Imitating the
Little Engine That Could

WHEN WE BELIEVE WE CAN'T, WE'RE RIGHT. When we believe we can, we are also right. Remember the children's book *The Little Engine That Could*? It's about a little engine who succeeded in pulling a train up a steep hill where other, larger, engines had failed. The little engine made it to the top because she kept repeating to herself, as she struggled, "I think I can, I think I can."

Tracy's mother read her the little engine book often because, as a child, she had the crippling habit of saying, "I can't." As an adult, like many of us, she sometimes regressed to that old pattern. One day, upon returning from a week out of town, she found herself feeling extremely stressed, almost paralyzed by the amount of work waiting for her. She tuned in to her inner dialogue and found she was repeating over and over, "I can't get all of this done. I have too much to do." Her subconscious was getting the message from those thoughts, "Red alert! It's time to panic!"

Becoming aware of her stress-inducing self-talk allowed her to change it to, "I have all the time and energy I need to accomplish everything I want to do." She didn't believe it at first, but knowing the process does work, she kept repeating her new, empowering statement aloud. In the space of a few minutes, Tracy's body relaxed, her mind cleared, and she was able to work much more efficiently. And yes, she told me, everything eventually got done.

Although it takes tremendous courage to change old thought patterns, we can help ourselves do so by adopting the little engine's phrase, "I think I can, I think I can," when we feel helpless or overwhelmed. Keeping our self-talk empowering, not panic producing, helps us do what we want to do and enhances our peace of mind immeasurably.

I have all the time I need to accomplish
everything I want to do.

I can. I know I can.

Calming the Monkey-Mind

OUR THOUGHTS CAN BE LIKE A THOUSAND monkeys in a tree, swinging by their tails, arms, and legs from branch to branch, grabbing at each other and then whisking away. Monkey-thoughts especially love to dwell on fleas, those things that bug or irritate us— picking, scratching, biting at our minds until our feelings fester. It doesn't have to be so. We are in charge of our thoughts.

Because learning to be in charge of our minds is one of the most difficult and frustrating tasks we have, it is tempting to give up and remain at the mercy of limiting and fearful thoughts. It takes courage to persevere in taming our minds, but it is essential for our well-being. We need to believe with our whole hearts and minds that we can control what we think, and then practice that knowledge with diligence and patience.

So when we notice our monkey-mind concentrating on fleas, we can distract it with thoughts of bananas, love, or thankfulness. If the branch our thoughts are swinging from is perilous to our peace of mind, we can choose to jump to another more soothing one. We

can decide what we allow our mind to concentrate on, but we need to be gentle with
ourselves as we calm our monkey-mind, because doing so is a life-long process.

I am in charge of my mind.

I choose to think healing, loving,
and thankful thoughts.

I have the power to create peaceful thoughts
even in stressful situations.

Choosing "That's Good!"

NO MATTER WHAT HAPPENS IN OUR LIVES, we have at least one choice. We can either say, "That's good!" or "Isn't it awful!" And the more we can say, "That's good," the happier we'll be because resistance magnifies pain, and labelling something as "bad" is resistance.

Polly, eight months pregnant with her fifth child, fell down an old-fashioned heating vent one day while her husband and children were away. Returning home six hours later, they found her wedged in the vent, calmly knitting. When she realized she couldn't get herself out, rather than struggling, crying, or worrying, she had chosen to make the most of a difficult situation by thinking how good it was her knitting was within reach rather than how bad it was that she was stuck.

Most of us would be hard pressed to be as sanguine as Polly in a similar predicament, but we can choose to see the good in most situations. It takes courage to resist feeling like "Poor little me" but making a commitment to ourselves to choose "That's good" is a giant step toward having peace of mind. When we notice ourselves resisting something that's happening to us and denouncing it as bad, we can stop and consciously choose a more positive reaction or attitude. Optimism and peace of mind go hand in hand.

*I choose to look at things
with a "That's good!" attitude.*

I am optimistic.

I look on the bright side of situations.

Reprogramming
Our Inner Mind

IF WE GET IN THE HABIT OF ALLOWING our subconscious mind to sabotage us by nastily flashing on to the screen of our consciousness statements such as, "Stupid! You did it wrong again!", peace of mind will elude us. None of us would buy a computer which did that to us. Rather, we would want a user-friendly machine that says, "Good try!"

Our minds are many times more fantastic than the very best computer and we are their only programmers. With strength, courage, and persistence we can change our negative self-talk to user-friendly inner dialogue.

Nyla's therapist asked her to keep a little notebook with her at all times and write down every time she spoke badly about herself. Being resistant to knowing exactly how hard she was on herself, it took every bit of Nyla's courage to agree to the suggestion. But she accepted the challenge and was amazed by how often she criticized herself; it took about a month of committed awareness and writing to extinguish her negative habit.

Changing a long-standing habit, such as negative self-talk, is difficult, so it is important we have ways to remind us of the desired new behavior. An excellent help would be to expand on Nyla's notebook exercise. Since our minds work similarly to computers, it is necessary to replace erroneous commands with correct ones in order to get the results we desire. Therefore, after jotting down the unfriendly remark made to ourselves, we need to write the corresponding positive statement—the statement we would like to habitually tell ourselves.

Immediately replacing a negative statement with a positive one is a powerful assistance in facilitating change. Peace of mind is a result of peaceful thoughts.

I speak to myself in a loving and supportive way.

I fill my mind with peaceful thoughts.

Avoiding the Future Hole

ONE OF THE QUICKEST WAYS TO DISTURB peace of mind is to worry about the future. I call this falling in the future hole. Future hole self-talk statements often begin with: "What if...," "I couldn't handle it if...," "I'm afraid that...." It's times like these when we need to remember the biblical observation: "Sufficient unto the day is the trouble therein." We can handle what comes our way today, but if we add what might happen tomorrow or two years from now we are seriously jeopardizing our peace of mind.

When Ginny suddenly found herself single after a long marriage, the hardest times she had were when she allowed her mind to project into the future. "What if I can't make any money?" "I couldn't handle it if my kids decided to live with their dad." "I'm afraid I'll always be alone." Falling in the future hole always landed her in the pits.

If we find ourselves worrying about the future, we need to pull our mind back to today, telling ourselves, "I can handle today, right now, this minute. Tomorrow is not here. Now is all I need to be concerned with." Gently

bring your thoughts back to the now if they
fall into the future hole again.

plan for the future but not
causes secure feelings; worry-
n. Planning is empowering;
imizing.

I plan for the future but live in the now.

*I have the courage to handle anything
that comes my way today.*

*I trust my life (this situation) is unfolding
in the perfect, right way.*

Keeping Afloat
through Forgiveness

LIFE JACKETS SAVE OUR LIVES BY SUPPORT-
ing us when we are tossed into stormy seas
and are just too tired to tread water. Without
a life jacket many unfortunate sailors would
drown before they could be rescued.

As we sail through life, we all encounter
storms and feel engulfed by tides of emotion.
Forgiveness, or an intention to forgive, is one
of our most buoyant life jackets. Others will
surely disappoint or hurt us on occasion,
whether intentionally or uninten-
tionally. And we will do the same to them.
Having the courage and willingness to forgive our own and other's shortcomings is an
unfailing life jacket—truly a life preserver—
keeping us afloat.

Forgiveness is a process. First we need to
feel and express our hurt, confusion, or anger
constructively. When we are in the midst of
externalizing our pain, we will not feel at all
forgiving. That's perfectly okay and totally
appropriate. However, it takes courage to resist the temptation to stay mad or hurt. At

some point, for our own peace of mind, we need to forgive. Knowing our goal is forgiveness gives us support and direction as we move through and let go of difficult feelings.

As we navigate turbulent emotional waters, the intention to forgive is our ballast. Being unwilling to forgive is like a weight around our necks, submerging us even in the calmest seas. Forgiveness keeps us afloat.

I allow myself to express my pain constructively.

I have the courage to forgive myself and others.

I accept forgiveness from myself and others.

Accepting the Unacceptable

THERE ARE TIMES WHEN WE ARE CALLED upon to have the courage to accept things that seem totally unacceptable—the death of a child, divorce, cancer, loss of a job, fire, etc.—and we wonder if we are strong enough to face it. Accepting tragedy is difficult and painful. And it is natural and even wise to rail against God or fate when we feel enraged and impotent, because that is part of the process of moving toward accepting the unacceptable. But in order to truly heal from an emotional, physical, or spiritual wound we need to stop resisting the fact that it happened. For resistance magnifies pain.

To help us accept the unacceptable, we can visualize life as an immense and magnificent tapestry. Having our nose pressed against the "Now" section of the pattern, we can't see the whole—and sometimes even the part—very clearly. When something happens that we feel is unacceptable, we can try to remind ourselves that at this close range we can't see how this fits into the pattern of our life and trust that, when we can step back and see the whole, this situation will somehow add to our growth and enhance the beauty of the entire tapestry.

Maybe we will never see the reason or the beauty in this life, but we need to trust in the benevolence of the Universe and God and, especially in challenging times, try to believe that eventually the veil will be parted and we will understand.

Accepting the unacceptable is extremely difficult, and because of that, we need to be very gentle with ourselves as we attempt to do it. Releasing resistance opens the door to acceptance and serenity.

God, grant me the serenity to accept the things
I cannot change, the courage to change the things
I can, and the wisdom to know the difference.

A Woman Has the Courage to Tame and Transform Her Dragons

When we face our fears and let ourselves know our connection to the power that is in us and beyond us, we learn courage.

—Anne Wilson Schaef

Often we feel we have terrifying, fire-breathing dragons zealously keeping us from the path to self-esteem and happiness. A great majority of these beasts, hatching and gaining strength in the dark caves of our subconscious, are generated by fear. Fear is the single most limiting factor in our lives. It binds us to hurts of the past and barricades our path to a fulfilled future.

It takes tremendous courage to extricate ourselves from the clutches of our fear-filled and limiting inner dragons, but when we fail to look at them directly, they gain strength. Growing quietly away from the light, they eventually rise up threateningly to demand our attention.

Freedom comes from having the courage to know that fear is not to be avoided, but faced, lived through, and learned from. Every time we face a fear and walk into the middle of it with support from others, a little bit is dissipated. Continually having the courage to face the internal dragons of our fears frees us from living reactively and gives us the opportunity to be who we truly are.

Facing the Dragons of Fear

ROBERT FROST ONCE SAID, "THE BEST WAY out is through" and nowhere is that more true than with fears. In fact, the only way out is through. When we run away from fear, it ends up running us! Unhealed fear acts as a fog, shrouding from view our myriad possibilities. Fear also is a magnet, drawing to us that which we fear.

Angie's fear that her husband would leave her was so deep she could not leave the room at night without him. If she wanted to go to sleep before he was ready for bed, she curled up at his feet. Her husband was devoted to her, and she could not understand why she was so afraid of being abandoned. She was terrified to look for the origin of her seemingly groundless fear, and her terror was justified. Wisely, she asked a therapist to be with her on her journey toward healing.

As she had the courage to look inside, Angie remembered an extremely abusive relationship with her father culminating in his disappearance when she was seven. As a little girl, she feared her father treated her badly because she was bad. When he left, she believed he had done so merely to be away from her. Consequently, as an adult, she carried inside her a deeply embedded fear that she was not worthy of love—especially from men.

Thankfully, most of our fears have less traumatic beginnings than Angie's, but if we are grappling with debilitating fears or fears we cannot understand, it is important we have the courage to explore them with a qualified person whom we trust and with whom we feel safe.

When examining fears we feel capable of handling alone, it is helpful to sit quietly and think of something or someone we fear. Then ask ourselves, "Why do I feel scared?" "What is the worst thing that could happen if I faced this fear and moved through it?" "Could I survive my imagined consequence?" Often our answer will be yes, if we have the courage to take it one day, one hour, one minute at a time.

I am willing to face my fear of＿＿＿＿＿.

I have the courage to face my fear of＿＿＿＿＿.

Rejecting the
Rejection Dragon

ALL OF US ARE AFRAID OF REJECTION. WE are much more susceptible to this fear when we feel we are unlovable. And how often do we allow ourselves to acknowledge how lovable we really are?

Marie lives in constant fear that her lover will reject her even though he assures her he loves her deeply. I asked her why she harbored this fear and her rather sheepish answer was, "Well, I don't think I'm very lovable." Hopefully, Marie will be able to change her feelings about herself. If she doesn't, she is likely to begin acting unlovable in order to stay congruent with her belief system. Without being able to view herself as lovable, she may actually drive her lover away.

When we feel unlovable, it is the wounded little girl in us who is hurting—the little girl inside who was either told or told herself that she was not okay, not worthy of being loved. Having the courage to love our own little girl is the primary step toward allowing others to find us lovable.

In order to help heal your wounded inner child, close your eyes and imagine yourself in a beautiful, protected environment. Visualize your little girl in this safe place with you. Become as open and loving toward her as you can. Reassure her that she is lovable and acceptable by telling her all of the things you like about her.

If you can't feel supportive and accepting of her, invite into the scene a compassionate mother figure who can love her unconditionally, and allow that woman to hold and comfort her. Realizing and accepting the fact that we are worthy of love is the best way for us to tame the Rejection Dragon.

I see myself through loving and accepting eyes.

I love myself and allow others to love me also.

Knowing We Can

I GREW UP WITH A FRIEND WHO WAS BORN with one arm missing from the elbow down. Before every adventure we were planning, I would ask her, "Do you think you'll be able to do this?" Her answer was almost always a resounding, "If you can do it, I can too." And she did.

Most of our limitations are self-imposed. When we know we can do or be something, we generally can. But knowing is not the same as wishful thinking. Wishful thinking is passive; knowing includes having the courage to find our way over, around, or through obstacles we find blocking our path.

"I can't" is one of the most debilitating beliefs we hold. Imagine that something we want badly is on a raft one hundred yards from shore and all we need to do is swim out and claim it. On the sand are swim-fins and a ten-pound bowling ball attached to an ankle chain. We can choose either of these to help us get to the raft. No contest: the fins. But many of us choose the bowling ball and chain of "I can't" and wonder why we struggle and sink on the way to getting what we want.

What we think is totally within our control. It is wise for us to choose swim-fin thoughts to help glide us toward our goals. We can either sink with "I can't" or swim with "I can."

I have the courage to know that I can.

I am capable and creative.

I help myself achieve my goals by knowing I can surmount any obstacles in my path.

Sacking the Bag Lady

LURKING IN MANY OF OUR MINDS IS THE fear that we will end up an impoverished bag lady. This fear can exist whether we are young or old, married or single, wealthy or poor. Often this fear comes from a sense of deprivation, the belief that life is like a pie and there is only a limited amount of good to go around.

Laurie is a wealthy woman but because she lives in fear of losing her money, she never enjoys what she has now—today. On the other hand, Malia is a fifty-year-old widow with very little money who feels abundantly blessed by her children, grandchildren, and friends. She feels secure that she will always have what she needs and has an attitude of thankfulness. When she needs it, money appears out of "nowhere" to get her through.

It is important that we have the courage to face and exorcise the ghost of deprivation when it haunts us. We can do so by ferreting out the underlying beliefs that create our fear and replacing them with a belief in abundance. While examining our fear, we may discover an underlying belief like, "I never have enough" or "I don't deserve to have enough."

Self-talk like this reinforces our fears. Becoming aware of this self-talk gives us the opportunity to change it to empowering statements such as, "I am thankful for what I have, and I trust I will always have enough." When we truly believe there is plenty, we draw to us that which we need.

Life is not like a pie, but rather like a never-ending spring—constantly flowing—renewing and replenishing itself. We can live with a spirit of joy and abundance when we change our beliefs to ones of unlimited supply.

Life loves giving to me.

I trust that I will always have enough.

I am thankful for what I have.

Owning Our Own Excellence

OFTEN IT'S HARD FOR US TO LET GO OF outdated and erroneous self concepts and see how really excellent we have become. I know that's a tough one for me. On the eve of sending my first book to the printer, I received one of my old college transcripts from my former husband. My prepublishing nerves were already raw, so what I saw in that transcript—some C's in English—sent me scurrying to my bag of tricks to help dislodge the Fear-of-Failure dragon that was sitting on my shoulder smirking and wiping his feet on my confidence.

Wanting to recapture a modicum of confidence, I visualized the young woman I was in college and reassured her that she was intelligent and capable even though her English grades were average. Then I began to focus on all of the education and life experience I had to offer through my courage and willingness to write honestly about my own fears and transformations. I brought into my mind's eye memories of people who had thanked me for helping them. I then listed talents and abilities for which I felt grateful. Slowly I began to internalize the feeling I had much to offer no matter what grades I had received twentysomething years ago.

With a simple change of focus—from concentrating on fear to accentuating ability—we learn to own our own excellence. If our self-esteem needs an update, we can make a list of our excellent qualities and even have the courage to ask our family and friends what they find excellent about us. It is okay to believe in our own excellence.

I accentuate my abilities.

I own my own excellence by concentrating on the good in myself.

I have the courage to believe in myself.

Refocusing Our Binoculars

ALL TOO OFTEN WE WOMEN ARE OVERLY self-critical. We believe that it is more acceptable for us to maximize our shortcomings and minimize our strengths. We have learned it is not feminine to toot our own horns.

Self-critical people see their mistakes leaping before them festooned with neon lights, while their triumphs wither from lack of attention. They look at their real or imagined shortcomings through powerful binoculars and look at their good points and successes, if at all, through the wrong end of the binoculars. Failures loom large and ominous, and successes look like specks on the horizon, mere accidents of nature.

It is courageous to refocus our binoculars, to give ourselves permission to move beyond self-critical thought patterns and realize what fantastic people we are. We can learn to "SEE": Savor Excellence Everyday by becoming an honest and appreciative mirror for ourselves. We choose to focus on the good in ourselves, learning from the things we wish we'd done better without allowing ourselves to magnify them out of proportion.

Making a list of things we like and admire about ourselves and tucking it in our purse is a good way to help us reinforce change. If we notice ourselves focusing on the negatives about ourselves, we can take out our list, read it, and then add another positive to it. Maybe our positive will be that we noticed when our binoculars needed refocusing—that's a great habit breaker.

I focus on my positive attributes.
I like and admire myself.

Healing through Feeling

SOMETIMES WE FIND OURSELVES SUPPRESS-
ing or denying our feelings for fear others will
not allow, understand, or accept them if they
are voiced. Only through honoring and acknowledging what we really feel can we heal
and move on. Yet we women are often called
"overemotional" and "PMS" to discourage us
from sharing, or even knowing, our true feelings.

In the face of such attitudes, it takes deep
courage to allow ourselves to explore and express our true feelings. We can help ourselves
resist the seductive Dragon of Denial by reminding ourselves frequently that we each
have a right and a responsibility to experience
our feelings.

Our physical bodies offer good examples
of "healing through feeling." When we get
the measles or chicken pox, for example, we
feel sick for a while and then we become immune to that particular disease. Our bodies
intuitively know that to move through the illness is to move toward healing.

The same wisdom is valid for our emotional dis-ease. As we move through our feel-

ings, express them, learn from them, and allow them to heal, we become free of them.

I have the courage to know and experience my true feelings.

I have a right to my feelings, whatever they are.

I express my feelings constructively.

Rechoosing How
We Want To Be

A BIG PART OF OUR ADULT WORK IS RE-
choosing how we want to be. Most of us did-
n't have a perfect childhood. However, if we
are still caught in a web of negative behaviors
and patterns from childhood, we can free ourselves.

Until Janice was sixty-two years old, she
always felt defensive and guilty when she vis-
ited her mother. I asked her two questions
that helped her free herself from the web of
old reactions. "How old are you when you
visit your mother?" After a thoughtful moment, she replied, "A rebellious twelve!" My
next question was, "How old do you want to
be?" She wanted to be sixty-two years old and
sure of herself.

Knowing that the simple act of passing
through her mother's door dropped 50 years
from her age and catapulted her into the uncomfortable pattern of old responses allowed
Janice to remind her inner twelve year old she
was now an adult and had no need to rebel
against her mom. It worked. By the time her

mother died three years later, their relationship was clear and comfortable.

When we notice ourselves acting in ways we dislike, we can stop and consciously choose how we would like to act or respond in that instance. We are not chained to the past; we have the power right now to re-choose how we want to be.

*I can see old patterns when they arise
and free myself from them.*

*I appreciate the good things about my childhood
and let go of the pain.*

I have the power to be who I want to be.

Uprooting "Rootless" Fears

WE MAY DECIDE THERE IS NOTHING TO do but live with a fear that seems irrational to us and grit our teeth in an attempt to bear with it. But there is a healthier way for us to proceed if we are experiencing fears that seem rootless, out of proportion to the apparent cause, or have no "logical" basis.

We need to give ourselves a priceless gift: time to explore confusing fears. The unknown can be so frightening that confronting fears, the origins of which we can only guess, takes tremendous courage. But it is also freeing, for only when fears are brought to conscious awareness will we be able to discover how to heal them. As long as fears remain hidden we are held helplessly in their grasp.

Since the root of our fears most often lies in childhood, we can expect to experience childlike feelings while rediscovering them. Seeking emotional support at such times is not dependence; it is wisdom. Taking the risk and having the courage to examine our seemingly rootless fears is best done in a protected and supportive environment. Before we begin to explore our inner demons, we need to find a person or a group with whom we feel safe, people we can trust implicitly with our vulnerability. It is okay to reach out and ask for assistance. In fact, it's often essential.

I invite into my life the perfect people to support and nurture me.

I have the courage to explore my fears.

I create a safe and protected environment in which to transform my fears.

Escaping the Depression Pit

DEPRESSION IS THE CLASSIC DISEASE OF women. Depression is like a fog that settles over us, limiting our ability to see what we're really feeling. But when we change the first two letters of the word, we have expression rather than depression. If we don't express what we're feeling—what's bugging us—in a constructive, healing manner, very often the result is depression: the way women weep without tears.

Often depression is really anger we've turned back on ourselves. If we are feeling depressed, we need to check and see if, deeper, what we're really feeling is anger. Anger is natural—it's how we tell ourselves, "Something isn't right here." But too often, women are taught anger is bad.

Betty gave in to anger once as a preteenager. Walking into her closet one day, she slipped in a little puddle her sister had left on the floor. She swore and her mother heard her. Her punishment for expressing her anger was being forbidden to attend a dance she had looked forward to, and her mother wouldn't speak to her for the rest of the day.

Through this and other similar experiences, Betty learned to invert her anger to avoid rejection and punishment.

We are only really depressed when we're so foggy that we're not aware of our feelings. If we are aware of them and working them out, even if they are angry or sad, we are in the very healthy process of healing. Having the courage to overcome our conditioning about anger, and learning to express it constructively, are two of our sturdiest ladders out of the depression pit.

*I am a good person
even though I sometimes feel angry.*

*I give my inner child permission
to have and express her feelings.*

*I have the courage to work through
my anger constructively.*

Chirping Up by Looking Up

FEEL LOW SOMETIMES? CAN'T SEEM TO drag one foot after the other? The weight of the world perched leadenly on your shoulders? We can chirp up by using a simple body language technique. Because our mind/body connection is extremely potent, we have more power than we imagine to elevate the "down" feelings we experience.

If we're depressed, our body will read our mind and translate the feeling into posture— slumped shoulders, head forward, eyes cast down, draggy and droopy gait. The exciting news is that our mind can also read our body. We have absolute control over how we hold our bodies. We cannot sustain depression if our eyes are looking up, our body is standing straight, and our walk is jaunty.

As an experiment, assume a position that is depressed and down. Hang your head and let your tummy sag out. Check your feelings. Do they match your posture? Now get excited! Sit, or better yet, stand up tall—stretch to your full height. Hold your head up proudly and look up. How does that feel?

Our minds and bodies, good servants to

each other, listen for each other's commands. We can give ourselves a lift by looking up, straightening up, feeling up.

I help myself feel up
by looking and straightening up.

I am an up, excited, and energetic woman.

Feeling Worthwhile

ON OCCASION, ALL OF US FEEL WORTH less (worth less than the next person). As a young and neophyte therapist I was shocked when an older and infinitely wiser (I thought) colleague told me she was in therapy. "What do you have to work on?" I asked. "Oh," she said, "feelings of personal worth. You know, same old thing we all work on."

Her remark underscored the idea that, even though we might wish it weren't true, our work on ourselves is never ending. We are always called upon to have the courage to continue on our path toward greater and deeper feelings of self-worth.

We are worthwhile just because we are alive. However, feeling worthwhile is an inside job. It is our task to assure ourselves of our worth by the way we treat and talk to ourselves. Other people can be very complimentary and supportive, but if we secretly know we're worthless, their words slide off as if we were teflon-coated.

Mentally check your self-talk. Does it enhance feelings of self-worth? Do you treat yourself as if you were valuable and precious?

Do you make yourself and your well-being a priority?

If not, close your eyes and mentally step back from yourself. How do you feel toward "you" as you view yourself from a slight distance? If you feel supportive and loving, great. Tell "you" how much you appreciate her and how worthwhile she is. If you do not feel supportive and loving, bring in to the scene a wonderful woman (real or imagined) who does love and support you and have her validate your worth. Soak in her validation and claim it as your own.

I am valuable and worthwhile.

I treat myself in a manner that fosters self-worth.

❀

A Woman Has
the Courage to Be
Her Own Good Friend

When one is a stranger to oneself
then one is estranged from others too.

—Anne Morrow Lindbergh

❀

THE ESSENCE OF OUR TRAINING AS women has been that we must sacrifice ourselves for others. In doing so we often lose the friendship of the one person who is always with us—ourselves. A friend provides us with vital ingredients for a satisfying life—support, appreciation, fun, understanding, and nourishment. A good friend acts as a gentle mirror, reflecting our strengths to us with congratulations and our weaknesses with tolerance. Without friendship our life is flat and our path toward authenticity extremely rocky.

If we have the idea that liking ourselves is selfish or egotistical, being a friend to ourself will necessitate a change in underlying beliefs. Change always requires courage. Committing to moving beyond devaluing ourselves to truly valuing ourselves is a life-affirming decision. Having ourselves as a trusted friend is essential for joy, growth, and healing. We can become a loving and supportive friend to ourselves—a person with whom we are delighted to spend our time.

Disrobing the Inner Judge

MANY OF US SEEM TO HAVE A NEED TO punish ourselves, and there are no light sentences. Our inner judges sentence us to hard labor in the frigid Siberia of guilt for the slightest infraction or mistake. Such treatment is incredibly hard on our hearts and spirits. Overcoming the tendency to be too hard on ourselves allows us to continue to call on the discernment of a wise inner guide without suffering inappropriately severe self-punishment.

As a teenager, Amanda used drugs rebelliously and had been promiscuous. As an adult, she was the model of decorum. She appeared calm and assured to those who knew her casually, but her family, especially her children, knew her perfectionism all too well. She needed to be in control—everything had to be done exactly as she dictated. Whenever her tight ship sprung even the smallest leak, she couldn't sleep or eat.

She was being eaten alive by unresolved guilt over her actions as a teenager. Firmly ensconced on the bench, her inner judge continuously banged her on the head with his gavel. Only by being totally in control of her surroundings could she silence him.

In order to transform a harsh judge into a loving counselor and guide, we need to know what the judge is saying to us. When we are conscious of our judgmental voices, we can then choose different messages. Guilt and punishment foster fear. Tolerant and understanding messages foster learning.

Having the courage to disrobe our inner judge and lay aside the handcuffs of guilt allows us to be more tolerant and loving toward others also, which, in turn, draws more love to us.

I am a worthwhile and capable woman
even though I make mistakes.

I am my own best friend.

I love and appreciate myself.

Tending Our Inner Garden

GARDENING IS A SOUL-FEEDING ACTIVITY for many of us. We nurture and care for our flowers, vegetables, and trees by watering, weeding and feeding them. Often we talk to them.

Studies done using special photography demonstrate that plants react differently depending on how they are spoken to. When addressed in a soft and soothing manner, the energy around a plant expands and brightens, and the plant leans toward the speaker. But when a plant is spoken to harshly or approached threateningly, its energy field constricts, the colors around it darken, and it leans away from the perceived threat.

What kind of gardener are we to our inner gardens? Do we cultivate kindly? Prune with patience? Encourage and appreciate our flowering and our ability to bear fruit? There is no other flower like us. We are each unique and beautiful, worthy of the finest care. A compassionate inner environment allows us to bloom more readily and more exquisitely.

Gently allow an image of a flower to come into your mind's eye. Imagine this flower is a part of you that is thirsty for appreciation and care. See yourself watering the flower from a beautiful pitcher. Imagine your flower lifting its head to accept the refreshing sprinkle. Feel its roots thankfully absorbing the sustaining and empowering water. Soak in the sensation of being nurtured and encouraged to grow.

I compassionately tend my inner garden.

*I gently and courageously prune
limiting beliefs and actions from my life.*

*I appreciate the unique beauty
I bring to my world.*

Empowering Ourselves
through Praise

HOW MANY TIMES DO WE CONGRATULATE ourselves? How many more times do we criticize ourselves? Congratulating is energizing; criticizing is debilitating.

At the end of a therapy year, Meg lamented, "I haven't accomplished anything all year long!" From my perspective, she'd done amazing things and healed in wonderful and courageous ways. To help her change her habitual self-criticism, I gave her a sheet of little gold stars and asked her to make a list of her accomplishments for the year, both inner and outer, and to give herself a star for each.

When she came back the next week with the list, she was amazed at how many stars she'd been able to give herself. Having changed her self-criticism to self-congratulations, her attitude was entirely different. She laughed more easily and felt excited, energized, and empowered.

Being a good friend to ourselves means that we have the courage to stop crippling ourselves with criticism and learn, instead, to compliment and congratulate ourselves. We can make it a habit to "gold-star" ourselves and become empowered through praise.

I congratulate myself for the good things I do, say, and think.

I congratulate myself on the person I am, and the person I am becoming.

I deserve gold stars.

Accepting the Beauty
of Our Imperfections

If we indulge in the "comparison crunch," the victim is usually our self-esteem. There will always be someone smarter, thinner, more creative, prettier, or younger than we are. We're all filled with holes like swiss cheese, but our inadequacies are in different places.

Being a recovering perfectionist, I have adopted as my motto the disclaimer often found on clothes made of cotton or raw silk. "This garment is made from 100 percent natural fibers. Any irregularity or variation is not to be considered defective. Imperfections enhance the beauty of the fabric."

What a great way to look at ourselves! Our imperfections enhance our beauty. Not that we don't want to change, grow, or do our best, but by celebrating the fact that we are made from "100 percent natural fibers," we create a climate of acceptance in which transformation can take place.

Close your eyes and imagine yourself as a unique and priceless tapestry created entirely from natural materials. Admire your tapestry exactly as it is now. Your wise subconscious has given you a rich symbol to explore. Write down your feelings and thoughts about your tapestry. Give thanks for its uniqueness, and appreciate it as is.

I accept myself just as I am now.

I give thanks for myself and my imperfections.

*I give myself permission
to transform and beautify my personal tapestry.*

Waking Up to Self-Love

GENUINE SELF-LOVE IS VALUABLE, ALTHOUGH often rare. Self-love is not selfishness or egotism; rather it is the creation of a hospitable and supportive inner environment in which we can become our better selves.

The breakup of my first marriage was one of the most potent wake-up calls I've had in my life. Incredibly powerful, though painful, lessons came from my divorce. In my healing process, I realized I had lived with such self-condemnation that I had virtually made myself unlovable to others also. Wanting and needing love in my life, I made a commitment to start by loving myself.

Moving from a place of self-condemnation to self-love was a difficult process. It felt so unnatural to think of loving myself. But sticking with the commitment I made has reaped more benefits than I dreamt it would for me, my family, and my clients. Having the courage to open up to loving myself seemed to open my eyes to love that was always available to me but hidden from my sight because I felt unlovable.

The following exercise will be difficult for those of us who find the concept of self-love hard to understand or accept. Having the courage to overcome our discomfort and do it anyway can work miracles in our lives by creating a nurturing inner climate conducive to love, empowerment, and peace of mind.

Look at yourself in the mirror each morning and say, "I will be a good friend to you, (your name), today. I love you." Repeat each evening.

I am willing to be willing to love myself.

I am willing to love myself.

I love myself.

Receiving Validation

WOMEN ARE SO OFTEN TAUGHT TO BE modest and self-effacing that it is uncomfortable for us to be faced with validation. About a year after my first book was published I attended a seminar on writing. As we were introducing ourselves, another participant began to praise my book to the group. I was astounded at the array of feelings which assailed me as she spoke—gratitude, embarrassment, pride, intense fear, and the desire to Alice-in-Wonderland down the nearest crevice.

Like Alice, I felt painfully conspicuous, lost as to the proper facial expression or response. My body stiffened; my smile felt as if it were made from hardened wallpaper paste. I was terrified. Who was terrified? My inner teenager, who was saying, "Oh no! If they hear I am good at something, they will be jealous and not like me."

If intense feelings kick up for us in certain situations, we can help sort through them by asking ourselves, "Who is feeling this?" Then, being a good friend to that inner part of ourselves, we can ask her what she wants and needs from us right now and give it to her. In the writing seminar my inner teenager needed to be reassured that validation is not necessarily coupled with jealousy and rejection. She could be loved, accepted, and validated at the same time.

Being able to accept validation is to have the courage to be modest and self-effacing only when it is an authentic response. When we are successful, we can be fearless in accepting praise for the good job we have done.

I am a valuable and worthwhile person.

I deserve validation and praise.

I have the courage to praise and validate myself.

Replenishing through
Rest and Relaxation

FOR EACH OF US, THERE ARE A MILLION and one real and imagined demands on our time and energy and so allowing ourselves the necessary rest and relaxation is often difficult. One of the best ways to befriend ourselves is to make sure we listen to our body, emotions, and spirit, and give ourselves the rest we need to revitalize and recharge.

Cars often have a helpful red light that blinks, alerting us to low fuel. And when we truly listen to ourselves, we can also hear the message, "Help! I'm running out of gas." We may hear the message, and yet ignore it.

Being a good friend to ourselves means hearing and heeding the empty-tank message. We all need rest and relaxation, and we all deserve to rest and relax. In order to feel loving and be able to snap and crackle with energy, we need to give ourselves permission to snap, crackle, then plop.

Make a list of the activities and places that relax you. It may be taking a walk in nature, quietly listening to music, or doing nothing at

all. Having the courage to not let the demands of others interfere with our special
time is being a good friend to ourselves. We
need to allow ourselves some time each day
to rest and relax in our own unique way. Only
we know when it is time to fill up our tank.

I deserve rest and relaxation.

*I take time to replenish my energy
through rest and relaxation.*

*I am better able to love myself and others
when I am rested and relaxed.*

Discovering Our
Personal Diamond

KNOWING AND ACCEPTING THE VARIOUS
aspects of ourselves is sometimes difficult.
There are often slices we want to ignore or
reject. Truly accepting all parts of ourselves as
they are provides a climate in which transformation can take place.

One way to think of ourselves is as diamonds, many-faceted and meant to reflect the
light. We are each special and unique diamonds. There are no others like us. In being
good friends to ourselves, we need to explore
all of our facets, realistically appraising ourselves by looking at all aspects of our being.
Each facet, no matter how dark it may seem,
will reflect the light clearly when it is
cleansed of old wounds, beliefs, and patterns.
Celebrating the facets that are freely reflecting the light of our higher selves, and gently
beginning to heal those that we have denied
because they are cloudy and obstructed, requires great patience and courage from us.

To help internalize the symbol of yourself
as a diamond, gently close your eyes and

imagine you are at the edge of a lake. The surface is absolutely calm, glasslike. A small point of light begins to reflect off the water and soon becomes a beautiful, shimmering brightness resembling thousands of brilliant diamonds dancing on the surface of the lake.

Visualize the light expanding to include you. Feel yourself and the entire lake as one big diamond reflecting light and love to all around you until it encompasses your family, friends, and finally the world as a whole.

I value myself as I would a precious diamond.

*I gently explore all facets of my being
and love each of them.*

Asking for What
We Want and Need

WE KNOW HOW TO BE CARETAKERS, BUT
can we reach out when we need to be taken
care of? We women are proficient at giving,
but receiving often seems strange and, somehow, not right. Emotionally battered and
bruised from my mother's diagnosis of termi-
nal cancer, I dragged myself to a day-long
workshop I'd signed up for before her illness.
I was excited when an older woman intro-
duced herself as the author of one of my very
favorite books, a book that lifted my heart
each time I read it. Although feeling a kinship
with the woman and yearning to meet her, I
held back because I felt so drained—I was
afraid she might be turned off to me because I
was in such pain.

Finally I said to myself, "Sue, how can you
be a good friend to yourself right now?" The
answer was clear, "Risk! Ask for what you
want and need." Hesitantly, I told her how
important her book was to me and asked if I
could just sit by her side and soak in her
mother-energy since my own mother was

dying. Kindly, she answered, "I would love to be your mother today." I spent most of the day with my head in her lap. Having gathered up my courage to ask for what I wanted, I received more than I'd hoped for.

We all have the right to ask for what we want and need. Once we have the courage to ask, most people will feel privileged and gratified to help us in any way they can.

I deserve to have what I want and need.

I have the courage to ask for what I want and need.

I love and accept myself even when I am having a difficult time.

❀

A Woman Has
the Courage to Make
Her Own Choices

When you are in doubt, be still, and wait.
When doubt no longer exists for you, then go
forward with courage. So long as mists envelop
you, be still; be still until the sunlight pours
through and dispels the mists—as it surely will.
Then act with courage.

—White Eagle

❀

MAKING GOOD CHOICES IS ONE OF the most powerful ways we have to live courageously—to be who we really are. When we choose attitudes and actions that authentically express our true selves, we are inner-directed. If we feel the need to check with everyone but ourselves before making a decision or having an opinion, we are outer-directed. We women often have trouble with this because we've been led to believe that others are wiser than we are. But no one has the blueprint for our lives but us; so it is essential that we have the courage to make our own choices. Only then can we be sure that the life we are living truly exemplifies who we genuinely are. We need to gently persevere in believing that while not all of our choices will be perfect, if they're ours, they will be right for the process of our lives.

Cruising with
High-Altitude Attitudes

WE HAVE THE CHOICE TO LIVE WITH high-altitude attitudes filled with optimism, enthusiasm, and excitement or to mope along with an Eeyore attitude of, "It's not much of a tail anyway. . ." Do our attitudes reflect the pure, clean, and heady atmosphere of high altitudes or are they murky and smog-congested? How we see life is up to each of us. If we don't like the view, we all can possess the courage and ability to change it.

At times Eeyore rides heavily on our shoulders, pessimistically warning us not to be too excited, too naive, or too enthusiastic. Not only are such low-rise attitudes depressing, they're boring. We can change our attitudes by becoming very aware of our thoughts and substituting positive thoughts for Eeyore thoughts. We choose our attitudes.

Imagine yourself on the top of a beautiful mountain. Feel the air, so clear it is like a zillion flawless diamonds reflecting the glistening sunlight. Bask in it. Take the magnificent view into your body—feel yourself expanding and lightening up. Say "Yes" to life! Feel yourself absorbing and exuding optimistic, powerful, and loving attitudes.

Choosing your attitudes, whether high or low, Pooh or Eeyore, determines whether you are happy or not. Have the courage to give yourself permission to live high, lightly, and with a resounding "Yes" in your heart. It is our choice, for we are the only guardians of our attitudes.

I am optimistic.

I say "Yes" to life.

I am light and I reflect light to others.

Uncovering What We Want

TRADITIONALLY WOMEN HAVE BEEN TAUGHT to acquiesce to the wants of others. They come first, whoever they are. Most of us were weaned on the idea that it is more blessed to give than to receive and it is difficult to break the pattern of denying our own wants. Going to the opposite extreme by adopting a self-ishly militant attitude of "I'll do what I want and to hell with you!" doesn't get us the love and connection we want, even with ourselves. But there is a happy medium. A calm and cen-tered knowledge that it is okay for us to have wants is essential to finding the balance.

If we have covered up our wants for a long time, we need to start gently by allowing our-selves to take a small-step approach to honor-ing our wants. For instance, Sylvia is a movie buff. She loves everything about going to the movies. Her husband is much more selective. For years she wouldn't go to the movies un-less he wanted to go also. One day she gar-nered the courage to calmly and kindly decide it was okay for her to go, no matter what he wanted to do. That small movie-step Sylvia took years ago has grown into an innate knowing that she can make her own choices.

Making our own choices, and having the courage to overcome our them-first, me-maybe-never training brings freedom to our lives and our relationships. Our desires are valid and being aware of them is essential.

Sit quietly and think (or perhaps write) of a time when you deferred to someone else. Ask yourself what you wanted in that particular instance. Now imagine yourself making the choice gently but firmly to do what you wanted. If it feels uncomfortable, reassure yourself that you have the right to have wants and needs. Daily, practice asking yourself, "What is my choice? What do I want and need now?"

I have the right to make my own choices.

I have the right to have wants and needs.

I make choices easily.

Growing Up Emotionally

THOUGH IT'S OFTEN HARD FOR US TO give up the old habit of asking, "Mother, may I?" (or Father, or Husband, or Kids), we're living in an age when we have unprecedented opportunities to make our own decisions, create personal choices—to be ourselves. As we unravel our emotional dependencies, we learn no one can fill us with confidence, independence, and a sense of inner worth but ourselves, with the ever present help of God as we interpret Her/Him/It.

We may long to return to the fantasy that it's okay to be emotionally dependent, that some man will or should take care of us. For to really know the buck stops with ourselves is frightening. But it's also extremely freeing to realize we can be independent, confident, and in control of ourselves. We all are called upon to grow up, to assume responsibility for ourselves. As grownups we are better able to love independently, interdependently, and joyfully.

Having the courage to grow up emotionally, letting go of the myth that other people know better than we do, gives us a sense of freedom and self-confidence that nothing else can. Being grown up, in the finest sense of the term, is a powerful and secure way to live.

I am willing to grow up.

I have the courage to take responsibility for myself.

*I listen carefully to myself
and make informed decisions.*

Inquiring Within

. . . .

SO MANY OF US ARE IN THE HABIT OF looking "out there" for our answers, invalidating
our own inner wisdom by assuming that, in
some magical way, others must be wiser than
we are—even about what is good for us. We
become other-directed rather than self-di-
rected. One of the biggest reasons for this behavior is that we are terrified of making
mistakes. If we follow someone else's counsel,
then it's his or her fault if things go wrong.
But if we are to take charge of our own lives,
we must have the courage to inquire within,
find our own answers, and make our own mistakes.

So often my clients say, "I don't know"
when I ask what they want or need in order to
be able to make changes in their lives. To free
them from their own inner pressure to give
the perfect answer I ask, "Well, if you were to
take a guess, what would it be?" Almost always they have an immediate and right-on
"guess." We are our own best experts. We
know what we should do. We are only afraid
we don't know or afraid that our knowing will

be wrong. It takes courage to listen to ourselves and act on what we hear.

We can learn to trust ourselves by inquiring within. To practice doing this, sit quietly, close your eyes, and for a minute focus your attention on your breathing. Gently visualize your inner wisdom as a graceful butterfly. Admire her beauty, and encourage your butterfly to sit on your shoulder and whisper her wisdom in your ear. Be still and listen. We do know what we want and need, and we can have the courage to accept the results and the rewards of inquiring within.

I am wise and capable.

I am my own best expert, my own authority about what is right for me.

I have the courage to listen to my inner wisdom.

Stopping Borrowed Trouble

Being able to handle almost any thing as long as we take it one moment at a time is an idea we can accept intellectually. Yet how many of us gallop into tomorrow to see what trouble we can imagine there, or slip and slide back into yesterday to chew on its trouble? We need to make the choice to concentrate on what is on our plate today. Living in the now, borrowing trouble neither from the past nor the future, is one of healthiest choices we can make for assuring peace of mind.

I have a friend whose husband is critically ill and will, if he survives, have a long and tedious recovery. Whenever she slips into the past with regrets about what she might have done to help him avoid this illness, she quickly pulls herself into the now by saying, "I did the best I could. I will be even more careful in the future. I will just handle today."

When she begins to panic about the future, she allows herself to "wail like an Arab woman" and get it all out, then she says to herself, "I am thankful he is alive today. I will take care of myself today by going to aerobics, calling my kids, or going to a Japanese restaurant for sushi—whatever feels good. Right now, this minute, I'm okay." She is making the courageous and healthy choice to live in the present.

We all have the ability to choose to live in the moment, as my friend is doing. Broken down into minute-size or day-size pieces, even the most painful experiences can be handled with courage and grace.

I live in the present.

I can courageously handle anything
as long as I take it one moment at a time.

"This, too, shall pass."

Daring to Risk

GROWTH, LIKE ALL FORWARD MOVEMENT, requires that we risk, that we court the unexpected. Many of us avoid risking because we are afraid. Risking is scary, but it can also be exciting and energizing. Risking new ways of being can infuse us with enthusiasm and a sense of empowerment.

For many years the fact that her husband drank bothered Sadie, but she didn't dare confront him. Because he was neither an embarrassing nor abusive drinker, she rationalized that it was doing no harm. But it was. His drinking was making him unavailable to her and damaging her respect for him. Talking to trusted friends and going to Al-Anon helped her face her deepest fears. What if she confronted him with the fact that she couldn't live with his drinking anymore and he left or, even worse, ignored her important revelation, and she had to leave?

Courageously, she faced her fear of being alone and losing a man she cared for deeply and dared to risk confronting him. Because she had accepted the risk she was taking and practiced what she was going to say, she was

able to talk to him in a loving and constructive manner. He has now stopped drinking
and attends AA meetings regularly, and they
are happier than they've ever been. For Sadie,
daring to risk created a whole new life.

Risk may be scary, but it brings tremendous rewards, including self-esteem and freedom. We need to honor the fact that risk can
be frightening, especially to our inner child,
and gently, at our own pace, take the risks
needed to enhance our lives.

I am willing to risk even when I am afraid.

I am proud of myself when I dare to risk.

*I empower myself by accepting risk
as a part of my life.*

Sidestepping
Others' Negativity

WE SOMETIMES HAVE THE INCLINATION to feel hurt and attacked by the actions or attitudes of other people. No matter how removed they are from us, we feel like their target. But we can tame the Target Dragon by learning not to take everything personally.

If the check-out clerk is brusque to us and our first reaction is "What did I do wrong?" or "Why doesn't she like me?" we feel vulnerable, as if we've been singled out because of who we are. A healing understanding to come to is, "I am not that powerful. People are not always responding to me, but to circumstances in their own lives." In the face of another's negativity, we can have the courage to reassure ourselves by affirming, "I am not responsible for this. I do not need to take it on."

When we no longer feel victimized or at fault, we can choose to send compassion and love to the crabby person. Even making up stories about them can be fun and ease our feelings. "Isn't it too bad she is suffering from constipation today." We can respond to others' negativity in a nonpersonal, light, and even loving way.

It is easier to avoid the effects of others' negativity when we question if an action or attitude is appropriately directed at us. If it isn't, we can choose to sidestep it and let it pass.

I sidestep others' negativity.

My peace of mind lies in not becoming defensive.

I protect myself in negative situations.

Selecting Positive People

ONE OF THE MOST IMPORTANT CHOICES we make in our lives is our selection of friends. A single rotten apple can ruin an entire barrel of good ones. Like those easily spoiled good apples, it's hard for us to maintain a positive attitude and high self-esteem when we're around negative people who undermine our sense of self. Avoiding negative people allows us to seek our highest level of being, unencumbered by the anchor of others' negativity.

Sometimes we live with negative people—what can we do then? First, we must become very aware of our limits. What comments and actions will we tolerate? Then we need to clearly state what those limits are and stand up for them. Usually, when we are firm about an issue, others will act as we have requested.

For example, Gail's husband, Joe, seemed to delight in putting her down by making fun of her in public and verbally abusing her in private. Her self-esteem was in the cellar, and she felt helpless—until she faced her fears about being single and truly decided she would rather live without Joe than be submerged under his pessimism. From a deep sense of conviction she told him that he needed to change or she was leaving. He's changing. It's not easy, but he knows she now feels good enough about herself not to accept his verbal put-downs and has the courage to leave if he doesn't clean up his act.

We can all choose who we relate to and greatly influence the way they treat us. It is so very important that we select positive people who lift our spirits and enhance our sense of well-being and that we do the same for them.

I have the right to have relationships that love and support me.

I choose to be around people who lift my spirit.

A Woman Has
the Courage to Care
for Her Body

*To keep a lamp burning we have to
keep putting oil in it.*

—Mother Teresa

OUR PHYSICAL BODIES ARE INTERWOVEN with our emotional, mental, and spiritual bodies. Each needs to be maintained, healed, and honored for the whole to work optimally. Having the courage to accept, be grateful for, and love our bodies, no matter how they look or feel is difficult for many of us. But it is important that we befriend our bodies because they are the vessels containing our essence, the vehicles through which we express life. Without the cooperation of our bodies, we as we know ourselves would not exist. If someone gave us a magnificent, expensive car that functioned smoothly and got us where we needed to go in absolute comfort, we would take care of it—keep it clean, give it gas, oil, and tuneups. We have been given such a gift in the form of our bodies, which are incredible machines, more wondrous than we can imagine. They deserve our respect, care, and appreciation.

Stimulating Our
Natural Healing

We used to believe that illness was something over which we had absolutely no control. If we were sick or injured there was no choice but to put our fate in the hands of doctors. With research, medical experts now know that a patient is much more in control of her healing than was previously believed. Our attitudes, beliefs, and emotions all affect how we heal. Challenging the old beliefs that we need to turn complete responsibility for our health over to someone else is a courageous decision to make.

We are exposed to germs daily, yet some of us seem more susceptible to illness than others. Why? Perhaps those who get sick expect illness as a part of life or feel victimized by germs. If so, the message we are giving our bodies is that we fear they are weak and defenseless. When this is what we believe, our immune system will be less effective and our bodies more prone to disease.

Our physical bodies need encouragement and reassurance just as our emotional, mental, and spiritual bodies do. Whenever we feel a cold coming on or seem especially vulnerable to disease, we can have the courage to feel empowered rather than victimized by immediately thanking our body for its incredible immune system. We can picture our resourceful white blood cells easing out any unwanted bacteria and visualize ourselves feeling well and energized. Over the next few hours we should continue to thank our bodies for their wonderful functioning. Of course, it's also prudent to pop Vitamin C.

While not a substitute for necessary medical care, affirming health and the perfect working of our immune system is a powerful tool we can use to stimulate our natural healing abilities.

My immune system is perfectly balancing and healing my body.

My body is strong and resilient.

Encouraging Our Body

....

NOT PAYING MUCH ATTENTION TO WHAT
I was doing one day while making muffins, I
stuck the spatula into the running blades of
the mixer. Quickly the spatula was sucked
into the blades as were three of my fingers.
The poor mixer kept grinding away as I stared
in shock at my vibrating hand. After what
seemed like minutes, but was probably
nanoseconds, I jerked the cord out of the
socket. Now the problem was how to get my
hand out. I was alone so it was me versus the
mixer.

When I did manage to pull my fingers free,
they were the color of skim milk and each
had a large, deep dent in it. Feeling faint and
nauseated I slumped at the table saying, "Oh,
no." But deep inside my head I felt the message, "You can heal this now." So, as I soaked
my hand in ice water, I began to thank my
body for its amazing healing powers and pic-
tured my hand as it had been minutes before—pain-free and fully functional. I talked
to my hand as a nurturing mother would talk
to an injured child, assuring it everything
would be okay. I even kissed it, as one would

a child, to make it "all better." Amazingly, within two hours you could not even see the dents and the only discomfort I had was a slight stiffness in one finger.

Our bodies listen to us. We can help our minds heal our bodies by the way we choose to speak. And it doesn't have to be an emergency to use this technique. By lovingly talking to your body each day, you can help it stay strong and healthy.

My body is a miraculous healing machine.

I love and trust my body.

*I gently encourage my body
when it is in need of healing.*

Paying Attention to Our Body Wisdom

OFTEN WE PAY TOO LITTLE ATTENTION TO the signals our bodies send us. But when we ignore the signals, our bodies may grab our attention in creative ways. Chris was going through an extremely stressful divorce and felt depleted by emotional and financial strain. Through exhaustion and an outbreak of acne, her body told her to take time to rest and replenish her energies. She ignored its messages and buried herself in work and other commitments, pushing herself to the point of collapse.

Then a small cyst developed in her ear lobe. She ignored that, too. So her body had little choice but to send a more graphic message. The cyst became enlarged until her ear was a painful and grotesque three times its normal size. With an ear that big, and being called "Dumbo" by her coworkers, how could she continue to not hear what her body was telling her? Doctors said the cause of the cyst was stress. She got the message. As she began to slow down, her ear began to go down.

Since we often fear appearing lazy, it is especially courageous for us to follow the advice of our bodies when they tell us to rest and relax. However, we can choose to listen to and honor our bodies' messages. Paying attention to our bodies allows their instinctive wisdom to help us stay healthy.

I pay close attention to my body.

I respect my body and honor its needs.

I am alert to the signals my body sends me.

Balancing and
Harmonizing Ourselves

....

MUCH OF OUR PAIN, BOTH PHYSICAL AND emotional, stems from a lack of harmony in all aspects of our being. When we are sick, our immune systems are busily working to bring our bodies back into balance. When we are upset, our emotions are yearning for a sense of rightness and harmony.

We greatly assist ourselves in staying finely tuned when we honor the four aspects of our being—physical, emotional, mental, and spiritual—and give each of them daily, positive attention. If paying attention to our own needs feels self-indulgent, it will take a lot of courage for us to persevere in caring for all four aspects each day. But we can.

Some examples of positive attention to our physical selves are exercising, eating well, and sleeping enough; to our emotional selves are sharing with a friend, writing in a journal, having a good cry, and helping someone else; to our mental selves are learning a new game, catching that creative thought, and cooking a challenging meal; and to our spiritual selves are praying/meditating, appreciating nature, reading uplifting materials, and spending quality time with our kids.

Having the courage and discipline to balance our lives leads to a more healthy, harmonious, and joyful existence.

*Each day I give
the physical, emotional, mental,
and spiritual aspects of my being
loving attention.*

*I have the courage and discipline
to live a balanced life.*

I enjoy staying finely tuned.

Appreciating Our Bodies

....

WOMEN OFTEN HATE THEIR BODIES. WE have learned body shame from comparing ourselves with the flawless beauties we see in magazines and movies. We fail to appreciate our own inner and outer beauty if they don't live up to the ideal given us, in large part, by the advertising industry.

One way for us to escape the tyranny of unattainable ad agency ideals is to change our focus from criticism to appreciation. We can begin by concentrating on how faithfully our bodies work for us, and praise them for functioning well. Our bodies deserve and desire our appreciation. We have nothing to be ashamed of, no matter how we look.

Doing the following exercise takes a great deal of courage if we have been taught to be embarrassed or ashamed of our bodies. If the exercise is difficult, it's very important that we gently take one small step at a time. Stand in front of the mirror (nude is good, but if that feels too uncomfortable, don't do it) and survey your body. Notice the places toward which you feel particularly critical. Even if you don't feel this way right now, tell these places that you love and appreciate them. Think of specific things about these parts of your body you are thankful for. Say these out loud, "Legs, I am thankful you are strong enough for me to walk on the beach." Now do the same for your body as a whole, such as "Body, thank you for allowing me to hold little babies and pet cats."

In order to accept and appreciate ourselves as we are, we need to have the courage to give up our negative feelings toward our bodies.

I love and appreciate my body.

I am proud of my body and what it can do.

I am thankful for my body,
which is my vehicle for moving through life.

Being the Right Weight

. . . .

ONE OF THE BIGGEST TORMENTS OF MANY
women's existence is the pain of weight gain.
Our self-esteem can plummet as our weight
inches upward and we inch outward. In addition, we know we are healthier, have more
energy, and feel better about ourselves when
we are at our correct and healthy weight.
Why, then, do we ride the roller coaster of
lose-gain over and over again? Why do our
good intentions about eating properly and
losing forever those extra pounds often end in
failure?

It is difficult to maintain our best weight
partly because doing so feels like deprivation.
We reward ourselves with comforting foods
such as chocolate and starch, and when those
comforts are removed we often feel depressed.

Perhaps one of the secrets to happily being
our optimum weight is to change the plea-
sure/pain link-up in our minds. Do we link
losing and maintaining a healthy weight with
the pain of deprivation or the pleasure of
being able to admire our reflection in the mirror? Do we concentrate on the pain of giving

up some foods or the pleasure of gaining more energy and being able to wear different clothes? Focusing on the pleasure of attaining our goal, and not on the pain of getting and staying there, gives us a much better chance of having the bodies we long for.

Allow yourself to sit quietly, eyes closed, and bring into your mind's eye a realistic and attractive picture of the way you would like to look. Visualize yourself at the perfect weight for your build, age, and lifestyle. Enjoy the picture of yourself at this weight, begin to imagine all the benefits you will have from being this size. Soak in the pleasure that reaching your goal will bring you, and gently encourage yourself toward it.

*I concentrate on the pleasure
of being my right weight.*

*I appreciate my body
and take good care of it.*

Aging as an Attitude

THERE ARE THINGS WE CAN DO TO KEEP from feeling old. Exercise, eat well, have love in our lives, be of service. But probably the most important way to feel young is to remember that *age is an attitude.* What we think about aging determines how we feel about it.

Elaine, one of the youngest people I know, is seventy-nine years old. What makes her young? She is enthusiastic about almost everything, is still working at her profession, is sincerely interested in other people and, since she continues to be open-minded about new ideas, is learning fresh things all the time. Best of all she is fun to be around.

You might think she has such a great attitude because her life has been easy. No. Her first child died in infancy; three of her five other children had polio at the same time and one was left crippled; money has always been tight; and she, too, has physical challenges. But her attitude is "Aren't I lucky! Isn't it fun to be alive."

When we have the courage to move through any fears we may have about aging and find answers to the questions that bother us, whether they are of a spiritual or physical nature, we can then have the peace of mind to age with an attitude of gratitude and expectancy.

I love and accept the age I am now.

I feel vital, enthusiastic, and energetic.

I have the courage to face my fears about aging and share them with people I trust.

Highlighting the Positives
of Aging

THERE ARE CULTURES THAT REVERE AGE, in which respect for a person increases as the years progress, and older is actually seen as wiser. Ours is not one of them. We still generally subscribe to the youth-is-better conviction. Individually, we have the power to choose a philosophy where older, in fact, can be better.

Energy flows where attention goes and we are in charge of what we pay attention to. If we choose to focus on the negatives about aging, our energy will flow in that direction and become depleted. However, when we courageously choose to concentrate on the positives of aging, our energy will be expanded.

After I turned forty-five or so, I could have chosen to focus on the fact that "hot-flash" was a term I was well acquainted with, or that when I looked in the mirror my mother's face often looked back at me. Instead I decided to concentrate on the positive aspects of aging (or "saging" as some call it), such as having the freedom to pursue my own interests and feeling sure of myself, more often than not.

We can all choose where we focus our attention, and that will determine how we feel as the birthdays roll by. Sit quietly, close your eyes and bring into the theater of your mind a picture or sense of yourself five years from now. See yourself happy, healthy, and enjoying life. Give yourself the qualities you would like to possess, or expand the positive qualities you already have. Absorb what it feels like to enjoy those qualities. Appreciate yourself at this age. Now see yourself aging in five-year increments, and love and appreciate yourself at each of those ages. Enjoy the wonderful old woman you will become.

I highlight the positives of being

_____ years old.

I enjoy and celebrate myself.

I love who I am and who I am becoming.

Oiling Our Apparatus
Aerobically

OFTEN OUR LIVES ARE SO HECTIC WE FEEL we must cut corners somewhere in order to have time for everything. Exercise is frequently one of the things we cut. Yet, if we do not exercise aerobically at least three times a week, we are wreaking havoc on our bodies. Aerobic exercise is necessary to oxygenate our blood, revitalize our immune system, and keep our muscles healthy and supple.

Aerobic exercise is also good for the psyche. When we are depressed, sad, or confused, exercising helps us dispel the cobwebs. That's because one of the greatest side benefits of aerobic exercise is the reduction of stress. We can begin exercising feeling stressed and depressed, and end the session feeling relaxed and alert through the body's release of its natural tranquilizers.

When our bodies are fit, well-oiled with exercise, everything else becomes easier. Starting small is important so that we do not get discouraged—we can take a ten-minute walk, or ride a bike for five minutes—and, if possible, it's good to make a pact with a friend in order to support and encourage each other. The hardest part of exercising consistently is initially making the decision, and then setting aside the time in our schedule. Chances are, if we can stick to an exercise program for six months, we'll be so happy with how we feel, that we'll be hooked—and healthier—for life. Although it can be difficult, being kind to ourselves by having the courage to commit to an aerobic exercise program will enhance our health and sense of well-being.

I enjoy exercising.
I make time to give my body the
exercise it wants and needs.

A Woman Has
the Courage to
Communicate Lovingly

The bitterest tears shed over graves are
forwords left unsaid and
deeds left undone.

—*Lillian Hellman*

WE ARE SOCIAL AND FAMILIAL animals who need to reach out and bond with each other. Communication, both verbal and nonverbal, is the way we relate and make our ideas, desires, and feelings known. As vital as communication is, many of us have been trained to do it in ways which alienate us from others rather than connect us to them.

To communicate, as defined in *The American Heritage Dictionary*, is "to make known." Learning to communicate more honestly, lovingly, and effectively requires that we have the courage to make ourselves known, to be vulnerable, and to change patterns of communication that are not working well for us now.

Seeking to understand ourselves and each other—speaking without blame and listening without judgment—helps us develop healthier communication patterns and adopt ways to share, and even argue, that promote understanding and closeness.

Pausing to Really Hear

BECAUSE WE VALUE CONNECTING WITH others, women are naturally good listeners. However, as our lives become busier and more demanding, we may be tempted to hurry through our communications without taking the time to really listen to what the other person is saying. When we do not pause and absorb what someone tells us, we can easily misunderstand them. Formulating our own responses instead of listening while another person is talking often leads to confrontation, not communication.

Having the courage and discipline to pause and absorb before we respond allows us to move beyond defensiveness into openness and understanding. Reflecting on what we have heard gives us a chance to ask for clarification if we need it.

When listening to someone else, it is important for us to become aware of our feelings. If they are angry or upset, we need to take a time-out and blow up in private. It's good to give ourselves permission to react, but subjecting another to the full extent of our intensity isn't loving or productive. After having made sure we've heard correctly and become aware of our feelings, we can choose to respond rather than simply react.

Caring communication doesn't necessarily sail along smoothly, one clear and concise sentence after the other; rather, it lurches along, with hesitations and restatements. Pausing to really hear and be heard helps us obtain, through communication, what we intuitively know is best for our well-being—understanding and connectedness.

*I pause and absorb what people say
before I respond.*

I have the courage to ask others to really hear me.

*My goal is to understand
and have my words reflect what is in my heart.*

Listening Often Equals Loving

IT'S INTERESTING THAT *LISTEN* HAS THE same letters as *silent*, and yet it is so difficult for some of us to remain attentively silent while someone is talking—especially if one or both of us is emotional. We either want to leap in and defend ourselves or "fix" the other person's situation. It takes remarkable courage to remain silent in some situations. And yet it's vital. For listening leads to understanding and creates a bridge to intimacy.

I once received a letter from a woman accusing me of a thoughtless oversight. I immediately felt defensive and wanted to "set her straight!" Knowing it's better to cool down before responding, I waited to call her until the next day.

By that time I had remembered one of my favorite statements, "In my defenselessness my safety lies," and hoped to be able to adhere to that during our talk. I started the conversation by saying I was very sorry if I had offended her as that was never my intention. With difficulty, I remained quiet through both her silences and accusations.

Eventually her emotional gates opened and out flooded much hurt and pain. Only a little of it really had anything to do with me. The funny thing was, having been listened to, she was then able to listen to me also; through the encounter we both came to understand and like each other better.

Being receptive to the painful messages of others often allows us to change the situation and feelings involved. Although it isn't easy for us to listen to the point of clarity, it is sometimes the only way to transform attack into love.

*I have the courage to listen to others
even when it is difficult or scary.*

I love others by listening attentively to them.

In my defenselessness my safety lies.

Answering Silent Pleas

So often when clients tell me their stories I can hear their inner child silently pleading, "See me. Hear me. Hold me." We all have a little child inside who longs to be heard, understood, and accepted. Perhaps we weren't seen or heard as we were growing up and now look for that approval from everyone, from our spouse and children to the grocery clerk. But do we give approval to ourselves? Do we communicate lovingly to ourselves? Do we listen attentively to ourselves?

In fact, it is so difficult for us to communicate with our inner child that we often need to voice our pleas to a trusted friend or mate who will understand if we talk like a child. One day when Anne was feeling disappointed and hurt because her father had lied to her, she gathered up her courage and asked her lover if her inner child could tell him something. He agreed and, in a teary, little-girl voice, she said, "Daddies aren't supposed to lie to little girls. Little girls are supposed to be able to trust their daddies." He held her and agreed with her, and she began to feel better.

Listening to our inner child and sharing what we discover with someone who will lovingly accept our feelings is very healing. If that seems too scary, we can have a stuffed animal or pillow represent our child and hold and comfort it ourselves. To us as adults this technique may sound strange, but to our inner child it feels kind and nurturing. Encouraged to express her feelings and have them accepted, our inner child quickly moves through them. We all can have the courage to listen and respond to the pleas of our inner child.

By listening to my inner child I help her heal.

*I choose the perfect people
with whom to share my feelings.*

Blowing Up, Not At

BLOWING UP IS LIKE TAKING OUT THE garbage: Our minds and feelings create emotional garbage we need to get rid of. If we don't blow up, chances are we'll "blow in" and feel depressed, anxious, or exhausted.

There's an art to blowing up constructively. When our inner dragons have built up a head of steam, we need to blow it out, but not aim it at anyone. Being the brunt of someone's emotional explosion doesn't foster openness. So even if we feel the other person is "responsible" for our anger, it is important that we have the courage and strength of will to hold off when we feel upset and angry.

After one particularly busy Christmas season I was steaming over a series of small incidents. As I ripped ornaments off the tree (I was the only person in the family working, it seemed to me), my husband said, "Are you mad?" My emotional pressure cooker blew! Knowing a confrontation at this point would be disastrous, I ran outside to vent my anger. Screaming, crying, whacking trees with fallen limbs, I blew out weeks of accumulated rage and frustration. It would have been unloving, destructive, and counterproductive for me to unleash the full brunt of my pent-up emotions on my family. No one deserved that. Neither did I deserve the consequences of suppressing my feelings.

In order to stay emotionally and physically healthy, we need to empower ourselves by finding beneficial ways to blow up. Then, having vented our excess emotion, we are better able to talk our feelings through constructively.

I express my feelings constructively.

Each day I am more aware of my feelings and express them quickly and lovingly.

Giving Roses without Thorns

. . . .

WE ARE OFTEN MYSTIFIED BY THE REACTION we get to our communication. Other people may be hurt by things we say, yet that was not our intention and we feel we said what needed saying in a most gentle manner.

A simple but incredibly valuable tool we can use to communicate lovingly is an "I message." The formula for an "I message" is: "When you do/say (_____), I feel (_____)." The goal of such a message is to express real feelings, not judgments or accusations. Using one or two words to describe a feeling is most effective. Examples of feelings: "hurt," "confused," "tired," "angry," "joyful," "uncomfortable," "abandoned," "excited." Feelings describe what's happening to us, rather than a judgment about whatever the other person is doing. Here's an example of a clear "I message": "When you talk to me in that tone of voice, I feel hurt and angry."

By contrast, "you messages" point fingers, make judgments, criticize personally, and interpret. The "I message" above could have been sent as a "you message": "When you talk to me in that tone of voice, you're doing it just to hurt me!" or "You make me feel awful. You hurt me!" The silent thorn at the end of a "you message" is "You bastard, you."

It takes courage to use "I messages" because we are laying our feelings on the line. If someone is really out to get us, they can use our feelings against us. Usually, however, when a person is not under attack from us, he or she can respond positively.

"I messages" are roses that inform and foster clarity. "You messages" have thorns that wound.

I am aware of what I feel.

I keep my communication clear by using "I messages."

I communicate how I feel without judging others.

Agreeing on the Right Time

....

MANY OF US RUIN THE CHANCE FOR constructive communication by choosing the wrong time to speak. Those four little words, "We need to talk," strike terror in the hearts of people who aren't ready to talk. And if we add "Now!" we're setting ourselves up to be met defensively. It's an absolute must that both parties agree willingly on a time to talk. Forced communication is often half-baked or boils over.

In Jane's family, they've evolved a system that works for them. If Jane wants to talk to her husband, she tells him she needs to talk sometime within the next 24 hours. She lets him know the subject—briefly, limiting herself to one or two sentences, maximum. Then she tells him just how big a deal the subject is for her. This gives him time to think about her topic and, since he can choose the time, which needs to be mutually agreeable, he has a sense of participating in the process. If she were to jump at him and demand they talk "right now," he'd feel attacked and defensive.

When we are in emotional pain—feel misunderstood or need clarification—it is hard to wait for resolution. We want whatever feels broken to be fixed instantly. Therefore, it takes courage to patiently allow another to choose a time that works for him or her. But is it worth it because loving communication feels mutual, and agreeing on timing helps create mutuality.

I trust myself to know
what and when I need to communicate.

I can wait patiently
for the right time to communicate with others.

I work with others
to agree on the best time for discussions.

Speaking Gently and Carrying a Soft Feather

....

WHY DO YOU SUPPOSE SO MANY OF US feel the necessity to hide our true beliefs and feelings behind socially acceptable masks? We are afraid to expose our soft, vulnerable underbellies to criticism, judgment, or insensitivity. Words can be wounding. Blurting out unedited, hurtful "truths" is unloving communication. Carole, a friend of mine, is a motivational speaker. Someone once told her, "My husband saw you on TV and was surprised at how much your face sags!" Needless to say, Carole felt hurt.

What was the real feeling of the person who commented on Carole's TV appearance—jealousy, envy?—I don't know. But if she had been able to use an "I message" such as "When I saw you on TV, I felt jealous," Carole could have understood and felt safe with her. As it was, she felt bludgeoned and sledgehammered rather than gently touched with a soft feather.

If we are to live lovingly with others, we cannot hurt them by sacrificing compassion for "truth." It is important that we have the courage to be truthful about our feelings, but it's a good idea for us to pause before we speak and ask ourselves, "Is this a feeling or a judgment?" If it is a true feeling such as sadness, anger, rejection, joy, passion, etc., we can then ask ourselves, "What is the most gentle and loving way I can share this feeling? What soft feather can I use to get my feeling heard?"

Thinking before we speak is a loving form of self control from which we can all benefit.

I am gentle with myself and others.

I have the courage to share my true feelings gently and with love.

I speak to others the way I would want them to speak to me.

Kissing a Frog

WE HAVE SO MUCH POWER AT THE TIP of our tongues. We can use words that empower, encourage, and support, or we can break spirits with criticism, judgments, and put-downs. Criticism wounds; praise empowers. It takes such courage and self-control for us to monitor our thoughts and words toward ourselves and others, but it is worth the effort. In a balmy climate of support and praise, we can help ourselves and others grow to our and their potential and beyond. However, in a harsh and buffeting environment of criticism, most of us wither and fail to thrive.

Remember the story of the brave and compassionate princess who had the courage to kiss a frog? Because of her willingness to accept him as he appeared, the frog was able to become who he truly was—a handsome prince. Daily we make the choice—shall we kiss our inner frogs and the inner frogs of others with praise, or crush them with criticism?

Of course our praise must be genuine. But there is almost always something we can truly appreciate about ourselves or someone else. It is often a matter of refocusing our attention.

We need to have the courage to recognize the vulnerability in those around us and look for the good in them. As we accentuate what we do like rather than concentrating on what we don't like about ourselves and others, we create a climate of transformation in which we can shed our frog-suits.

*I let critical thoughts drift effortlessly
out of my mind and replace them
with thoughts of support and good will.*

I focus on the good in myself and others.

*I see the princess or prince
behind my own and others' frogs.*

Honoring Ourselves
by Speaking Out

A UNIVERSAL DIFFICULTY WE WOMEN have is learning to have the courage to say what we think if it means risking disapproval.

For years I was so afraid of rejection that I swallowed my opinions, ideas, and resentments in order to avoid upsetting anyone. As I began to have the courage to be myself, I spoke out more often. Since we all have a tendency to resist change, my new habit sometimes did not sit well with others.

I remember the exact day my courage began to overcome my fear. My husband and I were riding our bikes along the ocean and had stopped for a rest when he said something I disagreed with and I stood up for myself—very gently. A few quiet minutes passed and then he said, "You're not feminine anymore. You have to be right all the time." It took every ounce of courage I possessed and a lot of reassurance to my quaking inner child to reply, "Honey, I've been right a lot, I've just never had the guts to say so."

We all have the right to express our thoughts and opinions, although others may not like them. While it can be difficult for us, we need to give ourselves permission to speak out from our hearts.

However, speaking out is not the same as shrieking out. As we begin to honor ourselves by speaking out, it helps to remember that all newfound bravery is sometimes terrifying. We need to resist the impulse to shriek and learn to speak out for ourselves in a gentle manner. It is difficult, but we can.

I have the courage to stand up for myself.

I voice my opinions gently, respectfully, and firmly.

A Woman Has the Courage to Develop Healthy Relationships

*Excellence in life seems to me to be
the way in which each human being makes
the most of the adventure of living and becomes
most truly and deeply himself, fulfilling
his own nature in the context of a good
life with other people.*

—Eda J. LeShan

RELATIONSHIPS CONSISTENTLY TEST OUR courage. Do we have the courage to trust others? Are we brave enough to persevere through difficult times, supporting and nurturing others when they need it? Do we have the courage to ask for support when we need it?

Relationships are a woman's lifeblood. We feel most alive when connected to family, friends, community, and the world at large. Sometimes, because the yearning for intimacy is such an integral part of us, we compromise in ways that are unhealthy for us. Healthy relationships are mutually supportive—each member giving and receiving, respecting and being respected. Rainer Maria Rilke writes, "Love consists of this, that two solitudes protect and touch and greet each other." When we have the courage to protect, touch, and greet ourselves and each other with love, our lives will be illumined by the light of rewarding relationships.

Drying out the
Responsibility Sponge

....

WE WOMEN HAVE BEEN LED TO BELIEVE we're responsible for everyone's happiness, moods, arguments, and failures. When our families aren't happy, we believe it's our fault and we feel guilty. I call it being a Responsibility Sponge.

If a puddle of discontent appears around someone, do we rush to their rescue and try to sponge it up, make it better, or get it to disappear? Most often attempting to rescue someone from their feelings leaves us with a frustrating sense of failure. That is because each of us is responsible for her/his own feelings and it is our job, alone, to rescue ourselves.

We have rescued because we thought it was the right thing to do, but breaking the pattern of being a Responsibility Sponge is actually very respectful of others. We are saying, "I trust that you have the strength and resourcefulness to work through your feelings on your own." Having the courage to dry out our sponge doesn't mean we aren't there for people emotionally; it just means we don't try to do it for them.

Because this is such a difficult change to make, it's good to practice by visualizing ourselves responding differently. With your eyes closed imagine a time when you would normally feel the need to rescue someone from his or her feelings. Very gently remind yourself it is not your job, that he or she is capable of self-rescue. See yourself able to be with the person, supporting and encouraging but not attempting to save or change him or her.

We need to be patient and gentle with ourselves as we dry out our sponges, for the belief that we are responsible for everything is woven deeply into the fabric of our lives.

I let go of inappropriate guilt.

*I have the courage to allow others
to take responsibility for themselves.*

Allowing Ourselves Limits

FEELING RESENTFUL AND USED IN OUR relationships plays havoc with our ability to be warm and loving. Most often we feel used when we have allowed ourselves to do more than our share. Why do we do it? Probably because some unhealthy and hidden belief, such as "I should be able to do it all," is running our lives. As we work at changing the underlying beliefs that cause us to disregard our limits, it takes courage to transform the inner voice that warns, "But if I don't do it all (or whatever our own nemesis is), I won't be good enough."

I once almost ruined a cherished friendship by overextending. For several years my partner, Bonnie, and I led seminars for women. It seemed to me that I was the one always racing around doing the legwork—making photocopies, delivering ads to the newspaper, and buying paper cups. Eventually I began to resent Bonnie and mutter things to myself like, "I'm sick of this."

Realizing all the extra work was not something Bonnie had asked me to do, I ferreted out the hidden belief that drove me: "Nice girls do more than their share." Wanting Bonnie's love and approval, I automatically did more than my share and ended up not feeling nice or loveable at all.

Becoming aware of the subconscious beliefs that prompt us to overextend is the beginning of freeing ourselves from them. Once they are discovered, we can consciously replace the old beliefs with more self-valuing ones. We can have the courage to keep reassuring ourselves that we have the right to have limits.

I have the right to have limits.

*I know my limits and allow myself
to do what is reasonable for me.*

Juggling the
Balls of Motherhood

STARTING WITH FREUD, MOTHERS BEGAN to get a bum rap. We were the cause of all stress and distress in our kids. Although we now know there are countless reasons children unfold as they do, "mother bashing" still happens—we especially do it to ourselves. We have an internal litany of failures, "I shouldn't work. . . I should always be understanding. . . I should be more lenient, or less lenient. . . " On and on we go against ourselves.

In fact, it is very difficult to juggle motherhood and all the other facets of our lives. We aren't going to do a perfect job. But we will be much better mothers when we learn to congratulate ourselves for our strength and resourcefulness rather than criticize ourselves for our real, or imagined, shortcomings.

Take a moment and write down your job description as a mother. What is expected of you? What myriad of chores and responsibilities do you handle each day? Pretty amazing, right? Making it a habit to congratulate yourself for the things you do well empowers you to do more things even better than before

We all thrive in an atmosphere of inner support and wither under criticism. Being a mother is a difficult and delightful job. Let's give ourselves credit!

I am a strong and resourceful mother.

I like my mothering abilities.

I forgive myself for the times I've parented poorly.

Dragging Someone Else's Leg Irons

....

ONE OF OUR MAIN TASKS IN LIFE IS TO free ourselves from the fears and beliefs that chain us to limitation—removing the leg irons that hobble us. It's a hard job and takes a lot of courage. Often we attempt to carry everyone else's leg irons also, thereby making it almost impossible to leave ours by the side of the road.

When we shackle ourselves to the belief that we must be in charge of everyone's growth and happiness, we create guilt and frustration in ourselves, and dependence and resistance in those we try to rescue. We only have the keys to unlock our own leg irons. To attempt to save others is really a subtle put-down. We are saying, in effect, "You poor thing, I don't believe you can run your own life. Therefore I guess I have to do it for you . . . sigh."

Freeing others from our over-concern empowers them by giving them the opportunity to solve their own problems. It also gives us more energy to work on transforming our own beliefs and fears.

Sit quietly, close your eyes, and concentrate on your breathing for a minute or two. Now run a little movie in your mind. See some people whom you want to rescue. Imagine them in emotional and psychic leg irons. Step back and choose to allow them to be in charge of their own lives. With great love and compassion tell each person, "_____ , I trust you are capable of handling your own life, and I now stop interfering by trying to rescue you." It's a good idea to write the preceding statement on a card and carry it around with us to reinforce our decision.

I trust and respect others'
wisdom and common sense.

I give advice sparingly and only when asked.

Mothering, Not Smothering

....

IT IS NATURAL TO BE PROTECTIVE OF OUR children, and essential—to a point. But guilt, fear, or perfectionism can cause us to be overprotective. If our children complain of feeling smothered, or pull away from us, we need to courageously scrutinize our actions and admit if we are being overprotective.

Both of Teresa's daughters live in earthquake-prone areas, and have gone through several small quakes as well as one large, destructive one. Teresa spent many a tortured hour caught in the grip of fear that her daughters might be injured or killed and that, if the worst happened, she, herself, would die emotionally.

Because living in a constant state of anxiety was destroying her peace of mind, she was motivated to change her mental images. Now, when she feels a twinge of fear, she immediately visualizes her daughters and grandchildren surrounded by a protective mantle of white light with angels safeguarding them. Then she gives thanks for all of them and for their safety.

Thankfulness casts out fear. The healthy

way to protect our kids, as they grow older, is to visualize them surrounded by light, love, and protection as they fly from the nest—for fly they must. We need to be gentle with ourselves in this process because to "love and let go" of children is one of a mother's toughest challenges.

Close your eyes and think of your children. Allow their faces to float before you. Do you feel any fear? Or guilt? Reassure yourself that you have done and are doing the best you know how. Surround each child, individually, with light or any form of protection that comes to mind. See him or her safe, happy, and productive. Give thanks for all the joys and sorrows you have experienced with them.

I love and enjoy my child/children.

I give thanks for my child/children and lovingly release them to their highest good.

Breaking the
Coffee-Fetching Cycle

RESPECT AND EQUALITY IN THE WORK-place are still elusive to many of us. Even women with tremendous responsibility in powerful jobs often feel the need to placate and appease their coworkers. Carrie, a brilliant executive with a growing company, feels intimidated by her male coworkers even though she is primarily responsible for increasing company revenues by millions of dollars. In her head she knows she deserves respect and equality, but often reverts to "coffee-fetching, needing-to-please" behavior. She catches herself assuaging male egos in order to have her ideas heard and respected, behavior she doesn't feel is necessary with her female colleagues.

Carrie is one of the many women working on breaking the "assistant" stereotype. It takes tremendous courage and insight to crack a traditional mold. No matter what position we hold at work, if we find ourselves fearful of asserting ourselves and insisting on respect and appreciation, we can ask the question Carrie asks, "What am I afraid of?"

For Carrie the fear was that the men at work wouldn't like her. It is important for people to like us because we are relational creatures who need connection. But this fear has a deeper basis, a primal suspicion that we need the approval and love of men in order to survive both financially and emotionally. Is it any wonder we learned to be subservient to men, to "coffee-fetch?"

We may have new beliefs about our abilities to take care of ourselves, but still act out of our ancient feelings on occasion. By recognizing our fears, we can learn to change our behaviors, getting coffee for others when we want to, not because we feel we have to.

I respect my coworkers and deserve their respect.

I am secure and capable.

Enjoying Self-Confidence

WHEN WE FEEL CONFIDENT AND SELF-assured, people are attracted to us as if we exuded a scent that announces, "I'm worth your attention!"

A vivid example of this scent-sending happened to Pat when she was in her thirties, single, and often struggling with poor self-esteem and fear of the future. She shopped at a neighborhood grocery store where everyone knew her slightly. On days when she strode into the store feeling confident and in control of her life, the Italian produce man would flirt with her outrageously, inviting her on cruises and moonlight strolls. When she drooped into the store feeling like a helpless victim trapped in a maelstrom of circumstances beyond her control, the same man would say briefly, "Hi, Pat, how ya doin?" and return to his radishes and tomatoes.

Confidence is contagious. Self-esteem is sexy. Healthy and supportive self-talk promotes self-confidence. We can choose to congratulate ourselves on our successes and console ourselves about our failures. When we have healthy relationships with ourselves, we will create healthy and happy relationships with others.

Visualize a time when you felt self-confident and full of self-esteem. Replay the scene several times and relish the feeling. Give yourself credit for how great you are. In contrast, remember a time or incident when you lacked self-confidence and were down on yourself. As if you were the director of a movie, change the last scene by acting in the self-confident manner you first visualized. Re-experience yourself as self-assured, capable, and happy. Notice how people respond positively to you.

We are the directors of our lives. We can choose how we act and react.

I am confident and self-assured.

*I like myself immensely
and enjoy my own company.*

Becoming Friends
with Our Lover

IT'S EASY TO FALL IN LOVE—OUR HORMONES see to that. But it's not so easy to be true friends with our lovers. True friendship is based on trust and brings out the best in us. Friends accept us as we are, and in that non-judgmental climate we feel safe. If we are to be friends with our lovers, we need to be able to trust that they will hold our vulnerabilities in gentle hands.

In her second marriage Joy, whose first husband was an alcoholic and unavailable emotionally, was often afraid her husband, Bob, would leave her. Understanding her vulnerability to abandonment, Bob reassured her he was staying and, even if it took her ten years to believe that, it was okay with him. Bob's understanding and patience promoted Joy's trust in him and she was gradually able to let go of her fear.

For many men, intimacy and expressing emotion is so difficult that it seems as if we are speaking two different languages. No matter whether we easily speak of emotional issues or not, we are all vulnerable in many areas. So if we want a close, fun, and companionable relationship with our lovers, we need to create a safe environment in which each feels secure leaping into the scary waters of shared emotions and intimacy.

Acceptance of our lovers as they are now provides a watertight lifeboat for the turbulent sea of feelings. Only within the safety of trust and acceptance can there be real intimacy and friendship between lovers.

I have the courage to accept my mate as is.

I create an atmosphere of safety in my relationship by being nonjudgmental.

My mate's uniqueness delights me.

Defanging Our
Expectation Dragon

THE DRAGON OF EXPECTATION CAN BE A destructive beast lurking in the background of any relationship. When we have rigid expectations of another person we create an arena for failure. What if he or she doesn't say or do the things we expect? We may feel let down and then assume we know the reasons for him or her not "doing it right."

Out of the ensuing hurt we can judge harshly or, worse yet, become martyred, sighing pitifully in disappointment, "If he really loved me, he would . . ."—a statement detrimental to any relationship. With it, we set the other person up to feel like a failure, an emotional incompetent. Tethered to the expectations of others, no one can fully express him or herself.

When we have the freedom and safety to express who we truly are, our relationships will be healthy, fun, and fulfilling. We can give ourselves a gift by having the courage to notice when our expectations defeat our desire for authentic relationships, and then work on letting the expectations go.

Defanging the Expectation Dragon allows us and our loved ones to flower in the safety of acceptance.

*I let go of any rigid expectations
I have of others.*

*I love and accept my family
and encourage them to live their lives
in their own way.*

I am okay right now, as is.

❀

A Woman Has
the Courage to Take
Risks and Change

Life is either a daring adventure or nothing.
Security does not exist in nature, nor do the
children of men as a whole experience it.
Avoiding is no safer in the long run
than exposure.

—Helen Keller

❀

WELCOMING CHANGE, AND THE risks that accompany it, is sometimes so frightening we are tempted to resist. Yet, as women cracking the traditional cocoon of limited possibilities and spreading our wings in flight toward personal freedom, we risk and change daily. Continuing to overcome our fears of change and expand our willingness to risk are two of the most productive and courageous things we can do to empower ourselves further. Being brave enough to embrace risk and change as inevitable brings us peace of mind and often makes our lives more exciting and interesting.

It's true that external change and risk, such as having a baby, going to school, or starting our own business require courage. But upsetting our internal applecart by uprooting obsolete beliefs, and uncovering and transforming our fears demand an equally enormous amount of courage. And doing so is essential to a self-loving, authentic, and successful life. Risk and change result in personal growth.

Becoming Response-able

· ·

OUR LIVES ARE NO ONE'S RESPONSIBILITY but our own. There are many things over which we have no control and for which we are not responsible. But we are responsible for how we respond to circumstances. And our response alone determines whether that circumstance becomes resolved for good or ill.

Often we react automatically by becoming defensive or shriveling inside rather than responding creatively to a person or situation. Thoughtless reaction rarely generates understanding or closeness between people. Since closeness is what we crave, it is advantageous for us to risk the change of learning to take ourselves out of automatic pilot and consciously choose our responses. When we have the courage to become response-able—that is, when we learn to choose our responses creatively and consciously—we're freer to build a life of continued growth and increased happiness.

Remember a time when your thoughtless reaction had uncomfortable consequences. Being careful not to judge yourself, because you did the best you knew how at the time, mull over other responses you could have made. In your imagination, relive the situation, choosing to respond in a positive, empowered, and loving way. Soak in the feeling you get from being response-able.

I respond to circumstances
in a healthy and helpful manner.

I carefully choose my responses.

I have the courage to think
before I speak or act.

Unraveling Old Messages

....

WE WONDER WHY, EVEN WHEN WE ARE successful and capable, we sometimes have the nagging sense we just don't measure up. We are probably feeling the aftershocks of subtle and not-so-subtle messages we swallowed whole as children—"Boys are better than girls," "You have to be pretty to be popular," etc.—which have become our own subconscious beliefs.

Without knowing it we guide our lives by these implanted thoughts. Because most of these notions are hidden, we're unaware of the extent to which they rule our actions and reactions—unless we consciously search them out in order to transform them. Having the strength and courage to find these underlying beliefs (under our conscious awareness and lying to us about our value) allows us to change them and continue the process of accepting our own inherent worth.

Take a quiet minute to jot down some of your underlying, limiting messages. How do you want to change them? For each destructive statement create a positive one that affirms the belief you want to hold. For instance, if we grapple with low self-esteem and fear of rejection, our affirmation might be, "I am worthwhile and lovable."

I search for untrue beliefs about myself and replace them with self-affirming statements.

I have the courage to know I am worthwhile.

I am lovable.

Releasing the Pain, Retaining the Memory

CARRYING THE PAIN OF OLD WOUNDS IS exhausting and burdensome. It's true that many of our most valuable lessons are learned as a result of pain, but it's also important that we ultimately have the courage and willingness to let go of pain. Until we do, true transformation is impossible.

I have discovered, through countless tears and heavy stones of shame carried awkwardly in my pockets, that it is important to release the pain but retain the memory. Retaining the memory helps us reach out in empathy, understanding, and love to those who struggle now where we once walked.

Sit quietly, close your eyes, and pay attention to your breath. As you breathe in, draw in a sense of comfort. As you exhale, visualize any pain, emotional or otherwise, floating out on your breath. It may help to give the pain a color. See, for instance, tiny red crystals of pain being released with your breath. Do this for a few minutes.

Now allow your mind's eye to create a beautiful, calm, and healing setting beside a clear, moving stream or river. Settle yourself in to a comfortable place beside the river, and give yourself permission to toss your pain into the flowing water. Watch it move downstream. Give thanks for what your feelings taught you and that they are now flowing away from you.

As well as visualizing this release, we can also go to a real river and use sticks or leaves to symbolize what we wish to release. Tossing these objects in the water and watching them, symbols of our pain, disappear is a powerfully healing message to our subconscious.

*I release my painful feelings
and reach out in love and understanding
to others who are in pain now.*

*I give thanks for my pain
and for the lessons I learn from it.*

Undergoing an
Attitude Adjustment

FACE LIFT ... TUMMY TUCK ... BREAST AUG-
mentation ... Many of us think of cosmetic
surgery to adjust what we see as our shortcomings. However, all of these procedures
begin to succumb to the law of gravity as
soon as they are completed. But we can get a
great and lasting "lift" from adopting uplifting
attitudes.

One of our greatest challenges in life
is to unlearn down and saggy beliefs and
opinions. We are free to choose our attitudes
and our self-talk. Circumstances do not dic-
tate whether our mood is up or down; we do.

If we are in the habit of walking around
with a little black cloud over our heads, we
can change it to a star or rainbow by having
an optimistic attitude. First we need to become aware of our attitudes. Are they positive
or negative, colorful or black, up or down? As
we have the courage to become aware of any
negative thought, attitude, or action, we can
write down their opposites—a positive
thought, attitude, or action—and then

choose to use it instead of our habitual one.

When we are aware of our attitudes, we can consciously alter them upwards. Deciding on an attitude adjustment is a life-changing commitment, a commitment to personal freedom, greater happiness, and increased ability to love.

*Each day I'm more easily aware
of my attitudinal habits.*

I have a positive, uplifting attitude.

I am an up person.

Exploring Our Shadows

IF WE WERE GOING ON A SPELUNKING (cave exploring) expedition, we would equip ourselves with a guide and some form of light, for in the total blackness of a deep cave it's impossible to see even our hand in front of our face. Interestingly, in this disturbing blackness, the light from a single candle seems much more powerful and illuminating than it does anywhere else.

The same is true for exploring our subconscious, something we all need to do. It takes courage to venture into the darkness, not knowing what we'll find, to slay the dragons of our fear and pain. Therefore, it is very important that we take a trusted light with us when we need to investigate the shadows of our subconscious caverns.

In order to move into the scary regions of our wounds, beliefs, and limitations we need a guide—someone who can encourage and uphold us when we falter. Therapists, friends, ministers, or support groups can help light the way for us as long as they are trustworthy and we feel safe. A trusted advisor can help us courageously explore the shadows and then emerge triumphantly into the light of emotional freedom. Although our internal caves are a must to visit, we don't want to get lost in them. Sometimes the smartest and most courageous thing we can do, on the road to personal freedom, is to say, "I need help."

I love and accept myself in the darkness
as well as in the light.

I have the courage to explore my shadow side.

I ask for help when I need it.

Leaving a Legacy
of Authenticity

....

WOMEN ARE PIONEERS. WE HAVE THE CHAL-
lenge and opportunity to make greater
changes in our lives today than ever before.
We are altering our roles in the home and
workplace, facing ourselves and our addic-
tions, and taking responsibility for our own
happiness.

One of the greatest risks we take, one
which is often painful and requires great
courage, is to relate to others—especially our
children—from the position of who we truly
are, not as an anonymous role made up of
shoulds and stereotypes. Through our example of courageously learning how to be and
express our true selves, we encourage others
to be who they genuinely are.

Each risk we take, each pain we heal, each
inner dragon we tame widens the path to
freedom for others to follow, and gives us increased confidence in our ability to lead authentic lives. With each risk we have the
courage to take, we make it easier for ourselves, our daughters, friends, and mothers to

summon the courage to risk being themselves. What more valuable legacy could we leave?

Relax for a moment with your eyes closed. Now see yourself approaching a room to meet with another person. At the door carefully remove, as if it were a cumbersome robe, any role, fear, or stereotype that could keep you from expressing your authenticity. Experience the freedom of relating from the center of your true self.

I have the courage to be myself.

I speak and act in authentic ways.

I trust I am capable.

Exposing Secrets to the Light

SHARING SECRETS WE'VE KEPT FOR YEARS is one of the biggest risks we can take. It is also one of the best things we can do to free ourselves to be who we really are, especially if the secret carries shame or blame.

Some of the unspoken rules in dysfunctional families are, "Don't talk, don't feel, don't be." As adults, not sharing our secrets (don't talk) often creates a need to protect ourselves by shutting down our emotions (don't feel) that, in turn, means we can't really have truly intimate relationships because we are not able to give wholly of ourselves (don't be).

Since that which we never expose to the light of reality tends to become unrealistically large and overwhelming, holding a secret, such as incest or abuse, in the darkness of our private closet can cause feelings of deep shame. In the silence of secrecy we often assume total responsibility for what we are hiding and torture ourselves with phrases such as, "If only..." "Maybe if I had been a boy, continued my education, stopped him from drinking. . ."

We need to find a safe person to whom we can reveal our secrets and from whom we can get support, love, and acceptance. When we decide to begin exposing our secrets to the light, we need to be selective and choose a person, or people, whom we can trust absolutely.

The courageous risk of sharing heart-searing secrets can lead to a wonderful sense of freedom when they are met with tenderness and understanding. Taking good care of ourselves as we expose our secrets to the light is a must.

I have the courage to share my
secret about_____ with an
understanding person.

I love and protect my inner child
as she risks exposing our secrets to the light.

Putting Superwoman
out to Pasture

I HAVE A BRIGHT RED CARD STUCK ON MY refrigerator that says SUPERWOMAN DOESN'T LIVE HERE ANYMORE. It reminds me that I do not always need to be everything to everybody and that the old workaholic, caretaker me is no more in residence.

Leslie came to me because she was suffering from depression. She still went through the motions of going to work, taking care of her family and her ailing mother, but she "just didn't care anymore." Not caring made her feel terribly guilty, which just increased her exhaustion. When I asked her what she did for herself in the midst of her demanding schedule, she could think of nothing. Superwoman was so busy flying around taking care of others that she was bone dry.

To heal, Leslie began to give herself permission to hang up the Super-cape and take care of herself by exercising, enjoying some solitude, and going to movies. The results? Her energy returned and her depression lifted. I saw her the other day at the store and asked her how she was. She laughed, "Oh, I'm out in the pasture happily smelling flowers with Ferdinand the bull!"

Do you have an active Superwoman who needs to be put out to pasture? If you are overtired, angry, depressed, or feeling used, the answer is probably a resounding Yes! When we do too much, take on too much responsibility, or overcommit ourselves, we end up being resentful and exhausted.

It is essential for our emotional and physical health that we change Superwoman behavior. Putting Superwoman out to pasture actually allows us to be more loving.

I take care of myself.

Superwoman doesn't live here anymore.

❀

A Woman Has
the Courage to
Recognize Rainbows

*The miracles of the church seem to me
to rest not so much upon faces or voices or
healing power coming suddenly near to us from
afar, but upon our perceptions being made finer,
so that for a moment our eyes can see and
our ears can hear what is there
about us always.*

—Willa Cather

❀

WHEN WE ARE AT OUR BEST—listening to and honoring our inner natures—we can tune in to frequencies within ourselves and others that are filled with the beauty, hope, and inspiration of rainbows. Don't we, when catching sight of a rainbow, automatically breathe an awed, "Oh!"? Rainbows are awe inspiring, partially because they are fleeting and magical. Even though they can be explained scientifically, they affect our hearts, not our minds.

We can all have the courage to look beyond the mundane to the miraculous, to recognize our own unique rainbows. Because I have worked for years with people who are dying and bereaved, and been blessed by their sharings, some of the stories I use will give you a peek through the veil we call death.

Recognizing Rainbows

IT IS EASY FOR US TO ARMOR OUR HEARTS against pain so diligently that we also close them to the appreciation of precious everyday miracles. I like to think of rainbows as God's equivalent to Hallmark greeting cards, a way of saying, "Hi there. I love you, and I'm around whether you can see me or not." Rainbows, notes from The Divine made up of light and color, are everywhere if we have the eyes and the heart to see them—a child's open smile, an unexpected call from a friend, a creative new idea, or the sight of an elderly couple holding hands.

Bonnie was driving down the freeway in Hawaii and noticed the cars in front of her swerving slightly to avoid something in the road. Thrusting its head bravely through a crack in the pavement was a flower! With misty eyes she told me she saw that courageous little flower as a rainbow, telling her it was possible for us all to bloom even in the hardest situations and most people can be trusted not to run over us if they can help it. It was a message she badly needed to hear right then.

In order to relish the rainbows of life, we need the ability to laugh and be happy. Freeing our spontaneous and wonder-filled inner child from the confines of "adulthood" will allow us to play more at life rather than working so hard at it. It is through the innocent eyes of our healed inner child, and in an atmosphere of spontaneous joy, that we can recognize the rainbows our hearts have known forever.

Having the courage to open our hearts to miracles allows us to enjoy and learn from our rainbow messengers.

Each day I open my heart
to recognize the rainbows in my life.

I bloom even in difficult situations.

God is loving me now.

Opening to Miracles

FREQUENTLY WE ARE SO "DULLED BY DOING" we lose our childlike eyes and are blinded to the rainbows of grace that come our way.

A short time after my mother's death, I was sitting in my kitchen talking to a friend about Mother's last few days. A moment after I told her that Mother had wished she could "fly away like a little bird and never come back," a tiny hummingbird came to the window where it hovered, looking directly at me, for several seconds. The hairs stood up on my arms and tears came to my eyes. I felt as if the little bird were giving me a message from Mother—reassuring me that "Even though you can't see me, I am with you." The adult in me could chalk it all up to coincidence, but my miracle-loving child firmly believes it was a heavenly love note.

We need to have the courage to go against the current of society which demands we do so much that we forget to be, and take time to open our eyes and hearts to the miracles that surround us daily. We can look at our world through the awestruck eyes of our inner child and be deeply enriched by doing so.

Today, as you go about your usual routine, try a little experiment. Look at your surroundings and at the people you encounter with the unabashed curiosity of a child. For a least a few seconds, see your world through eyes that expect a miracle.

I take time to open my eyes and heart to miracles.

I allow my inner child to revel in everyday blessings.

I have the courage to believe in the miraculous.

Focusing on Beauty

WHEN WE ARE IN PAIN OR CONFUSION and our minds stubbornly gnaw on the source, it is often healing to refocus our thoughts on beauty. Remembering to change our focus and finding the self-discipline to do so is courageous.

Janet was going through a painful divorce. Once, when her heart was ragged and bleeding, she sat behind her soon-to-be-ex-husband at their son's Little League game. Her husband and his girlfriend were snuggling and giggling throughout the game. Janet longed to leave but did not want to disappoint her son. Nervously picking at the grass, she noticed she was sitting by a clump of wildflowers that had tiny blue blooms. To ease her heart, she began to focus on the flowers. They were beautiful and delicate, each a little different from its sister, perfect. . . .

To Janet's surprise she began to feel peace seeping into every crevice of her being, and she felt completely loved. She realized if God cared enough to create the astounding beauty of those little weeds in the middle of a school yard, God must also love her, even in the middle of her emotional wasteland.

Mother Nature is healing. She surrounds us with beauty that can bind our wounds and delight our hearts if we let it. We need to relate to her—get dirt under our nails. Even if we live in an apartment in the middle of Manhattan, we can have flowers that lift their little faces to us in gratitude for the water and food we give them. The miraculous beauty of even the simplest flower can give our hearts a boost if we have the courage and willingness to take the time to really see and savor it.

Give yourself the gift of looking into the face of a flower. Take time with it. Appreciate the miracle of it.

*I fill myself with the beauty and
peace of nature.*

*I have the courage to focus on beauty
even in the midst of pain.*

Reaching through the Veil

DIANE'S DAUGHTER, SALLY, DIED OF BONE cancer when she was thirty-one. During the last few days of her life she was comatose off and on, so weak she could barely move. But one day she sat upright, looked toward the foot of her bed and exclaimed, "Grandma, you're so young!" Later, when Sally regained consciousness, Diane asked her if she had seen her grandmother. She answered peacefully, "Oh, yes, Grandma is waiting for me!" Grandma had died when Sally was three years old.

Stories such as these can help alleviate our fear of death and dying. In the very depths of our hearts we can come to believe we never die alone—that there are always loved ones and escorts to greet us. This belief can also help us realize we do not live alone either; there are always people willing and able to be with us and help us when we need it.

Solace and understanding are available to us when we have the courage to reach through the veil of our resistance or shame and ask for what we want and need. Opening our hearts to the awareness that we are always loved and never alone brings us the security and peace of mind for which we all yearn. The veil between us and the divine is more permeable than we imagine.

I trust I am never alone.

I am loved and protected in this life and beyond.

*I have the courage to open myself
to the love that surrounds me.*

Seeing with the
Eyes of Innocence

....

WHEN MY SONS WERE LITTLE I ALWAYS
tucked them into bed with a prayer asking
their guardian angels to watch over them as
they slept. As I began to learn about phenom-
ena such as ESP, near-death experiences, and
the wonders of mystics and shamans, it occurred to me to find out if they ever saw their
guardian angels. When I asked, they looked
at me with their innocent four- and six-year-
old eyes and said, "Sure! Don't you?" Unfortunately, no. I had lost my innocence and
openness to the miraculous as I moved into
the serious reality of adulthood. But my little
boys helped me recapture a sense of wonder
and awe.

Courageously allowing ourselves to become aware of our world through the eyes of
innocence—to grow young—opens up a vista
of external and internal beauty easily missed
if our nose is always pressed to the grown-up
grindstone. We can practice looking at things
with the eyes of an enthusiastic four-year-old
and experience similar wonder.

Sit quietly, with your eyes closed, and open your inner, innocent eyes. Invite into your presence one or more compassionate and beautiful angels. As you visualize these exquisite Beings of Light, open yourself to absorb the love, strength, and peace of mind that emanates from them. Invite them to re-parent you by loving you exactly as you are now. Allow yourself to become a cherished and valued child of these Beings.

I am valuable and lovable.

*I allow myself to absorb
love and acceptance from others.*

I have the courage to know I am worthy.

Emulating Butterflies

BECAUSE BUTTERFLIES ARE DEEPLY SYMBOLIC of our own struggle to grow into our unique beauty and wisdom, they bring a smile to our faces. As with the swan, which also grows into its beauty and grace, the butterfly in its immature larva stage is not at all appealing. But, following a deep inner knowing, it goes into seclusion to allow its destiny to unfold. Protecting itself from outside distractions, it retreats to the darkness and isolation of its cocoon. In due time, as promised by its inner wisdom, it emerges as a winged creature and spends the rest of its life spreading beauty and joy as it gently flies from flower to flower—a symbol of hope and transformation.

As we move through the chaos, confusion, and challenges of everyday life, we should remember we have a winged and wonderful Self within us, waiting to emerge from the darkness. Like the butterfly, we need only go into the stillness and solitude—to look within—to find our wise Inner-Self waiting to transform us through her knowing embrace.

Being gentle and patient with ourselves as we go within is essential. Transformation takes time, commitment, and discipline. Each day we need to give ourselves the blessing of a few quiet minutes of cocooning. We can have the courage to trust the cocooning process and not expect spectacular fireworks or even insights at first. It takes a while for our minds to become quiet enough for us to hear the flutter of our inner wings.

I trust my inner butterfly.

*I take a few quiet minutes each day
to tune into my inner self.*

*Each day I am more able to hear
the quiet whispers of my inner wings.*

Laughing with Our Klutz

IT TAKES COURAGE TO LAUGH, TO HAVE A sense of humor. Why? Because when something is really funny it is a reflection of our own foibles and weaknesses, those things about ourselves which make us cringe. To have a good sense of humor, we must be able to not take ourselves too seriously—to increase our ability to laugh with, not at, ourselves as we stumble and stagger through the comedy of life.

This is especially difficult for women because we have been taught that how we look is incredibly important. As girls we were definitely encouraged to be aware of what the neighbors would think, and that left many of us fearful of being judged if we acted in an unladylike manner. Becoming comfortable with ourselves when we have egg on our faces as well as when we are doing things perfectly is a challenge, but ultimately makes us more fun to be around.

Barbara was terrified of appearing foolish in front of others because she was afraid they would reject her. But that was really only her surface belief. Her deep, underlying conviction was that she was only lovable if she was perfect. When she began to change that belief by assuring herself she would love herself as a queen or a klutz, in strength and vulnerability, slim or chubby, she began to enjoy herself more. In fact, she has become so good at loving and reassuring her insecure inner child that she actually gets a kick out of her klutzy self now.

We can do as Barbara did. Instead of seeing our klutzy self as a part of us we must hide, we can choose to view her as a charming and irresistible free spirit.

I have the courage to take myself lightly.

I am a worthwhile and capable woman even though I make mistakes.

Putting a Little Play in Our Day

. . . .

ONE OF OUR BIGGEST CHALLENGES CAN BE allowing ourselves the seeming luxury of playing during our busy days. Play isn't necessarily a time-consuming activity; play also can be an attitude.

Jeannie works as activities director at a retirement home. In an environment that could be sobering and serious, she has decided to inject an attitude of playfulness. Jeannie cultivates her ability to delight in and lighten up the mundane and serious business of day-to-day living. She taps into her spontaneous inner child by trying to look at each day as an event to be celebrated. She dresses in costume (simple and homemade) for all holidays and sometimes just because . . . But more importantly, she allows her ready and raucous laughter to bounce uninhibitedly down the corridors of her workplace and her life. Jeannie is her own best playmate, and her example is helping the residents of her facility adopt an attitude of playfulness in their lives.

Reminding ourselves to incorporate an attitude of playfulness into our day can be done by putting little cards around saying, for instance, IT'S OK TO PLAY, I PUT A LITTLE PLAY IN MY DAY, or LIFE—FOR THE FUN OF IT. Often keeping ourselves aware of our desired change is the only impetus we need to lighten up.

Sit quietly (maybe holding a teddy bear), close your eyes, and invite into your mind's theater a spontaneous child who is filled with wonder at all life—a child with whom you would like to be best friends. Create a place filled with marvelous things to play with and exciting spots to explore. Have fun. Enjoy each other and your time together.

Getting in the habit of inviting your new friend to be a part of your everyday life gives you a chance to learn from her how to enjoy, to be in childlike joy, daily.

I encourage myself to play and have fun.

I am my own best playmate.

I enjoy having an attitude of playfulness.

Detaching Compassionately
through Play

MOST OF US HAVE OTHERS IN OUR LIVES, often family members, whom we allow to emotionally sabotage us. After encountering them, we either seethe with frustration or are saturated with guilt. Learning to compassionately detach from such people is one of the most courageous and empowering things we can do for ourselves.

Sandy spent years feeling guilt-ridden and frustrated over her alcoholic brother. He was convinced she had received all the love and attention from their parents and that her success was the reason for his failure. No amount of rational communication, refuting, or compassion changed his mind. She was always the bad guy in his eyes. Having tried many unsuccessful ways of unhooking, Sandy decided she had nothing to lose by playing at it rather than working so hard.

During their next conversation her brother's poor-me, if-it-wasn't-for-you litany began but she handled it differently. She visualized cartoon hooks flying all around her, and she whisked them away with her hands saying (silently, since they were on the phone), "I won't have any hooks today, thank you!" Sandy began to really enjoy herself, batting away all the old and ugly hooks that used to pierce her.

When Sandy began taking her brother's comments less seriously, she was able to remain open to him. Eventually, without her resistance to keep him fueled and fired up, he began to act differently. We can unhook from trying to change another person's mind, save him or her, or defend ourselves, and we can do it playfully.

I have the courage to compassionately detach from others when necessary.

I lighten up about things that irritate me.

Nestling in the Arms of Nature

THE DIFFICULT ADJUSTMENT OF MOVING from Hawaii to California was eased for me when I learned how to nestle in the arms of trees. The Sisters, as I had named two straight and regal pine trees at the edge of my new backyard forest, beckoned me to visit. But I was bustling about doing the business of settling in. One day, however, when I felt especially lonely, housebound, and resentful, I remembered someone telling me about the benefits of hugging a tree.

Extricating myself from packing boxes and pictures needing to be hung, I made my way through the blackberries and undergrowth to the base of The Sisters. Collapsing between them, I began to relax. To my great surprise, I started to cry. In the presence of these two trees, friends from the moment I first laid eyes on them, I became aware of feelings I'd been suppressing. Through my tears I began to talk aloud. A sense of acceptance, comfort, and peace floated through me as I bared my soul to The Sisters. I was able to return to my chores renewed and refreshed.

Nature is pure, patient, and nonjudgmental; she accepts us all, and we all need her acceptance. The love of Mother Nature can help us all when we have the courage to open to it.

Sit quietly. With your eyes closed, create a beautiful place in nature, either real or imaginary, and begin to enjoy the sounds and sights around you. Familiarize yourself with the area and then settle comfortably into your favorite space. Accept and absorb the peace and comfort of this little oasis. Open to the strength that emanates from both the living and inanimate objects. Bask in this beauty and strength and allow it to become a healing and soothing part of you.

I take the time to be in and appreciate nature.

*I am comforted
by the strength and beauty of nature.*

A Woman Has the Courage to Claim the Goddess Within

What woman needs is not as a woman to act or rule, but as a nature to grow, as an intellect to discern, as a soul to live freely and unimpeded, to unfold such powers as were given to her when we left our common home.

—Margaret Fuller

IN ESSENCE, WE ARE ALL SPARKS OF The Divine. Realizing this we can accept that the Goddess within each of us is not an untouchable, illusionary figment of our imagination. She is real, an integral part of us, the self that possesses what has been called "female intuition." Resisting and denying the wisdom of our intuition cuts us off from our most precious and feminine features. Thankfully, we are now reclaiming the Goddess within by accepting those aspects of ourselves that respect our intuition.

Until recently the Goddess within many of us had been silenced because we feared her power and had no idea how to wield it lovingly. Fortunately, we are now learning guidelines for expressing her power in constructive ways. Allowing ourselves to know and honor our powerful inner wisdom takes courage, for when we do, not only do we experience the joy of spiritual development, we also have the responsibilities that empowerment and wisdom bring.

We are all entrusted with the light of the Goddess. It is our birthright and responsibility to allow that light to illumine our life's path.

Training the Priestess in Us

MY DEAR FRIEND AND SPIRITUAL MOTHER refers to the challenges we face in the school of life as the training of the priestess. Somehow seeing our everyday difficulties in the light of priestess training lends meaning to their teachings.

We all have an understanding, compassionate, and gentle inner priestess who sits beside an artesian well of wisdom. We are in training to recognize and claim that part of ourselves. Being able to call her forth when we need her is to be in touch with our limitless source of wisdom.

Close your eyes and begin to hear the gentle bubbling of spring water. Allow yourself to feel soothed and comforted by the sound. Notice you are by a lovely fountain flowing with crystal clear water. Invite into this sacred place your inner priestess. If you do not feel totally loved by the woman who appears, she is not your priestess. Allow that image to fade and invite your real priestess to be with you. When she appears, spend some time getting to know her and exploring your beautiful surroundings together. She has a gift for you, a

vase you can fill with water from the fountain.
Ask her if she is willing to guide you on your
path. Agree to meet with each other regularly, becoming partners and friends as you
train together through difficulties, decisions,
and triumphs.

*I welcome the wisdom and compassion
of my inner priestess.*

*I easily accept the valuable lessons
learned in the school of life.*

I am feminine, in the finest sense of the word.

Accepting Our Credibility

HOW OFTEN DO WE HAVE A SMIRKING cynic on our shoulder saying various versions of "What do you know?" and "Why would people want to hear what you have to say?" Even in the face of compliments, honors, and successes we women seem to question our credibility. Our doubt is fueled by degrading self-talk and the flames of low self-esteem are fanned by repetition.

But we are in charge of our thoughts. Through awareness, affirmations, and healing—changing our self-talk and self-concept—we can diminish the judging voice from a shout to a whisper, eventually replacing it with a loving and supportive inner voice that believes in our credibility. With courage and commitment we can learn to give ourselves the credit we deserve, cut our self-criticism, and accept the idea that what we know and think has value.

You are incredibly competent. If life were a university, what degrees would you have earned thus far and what ones are you now working toward? A B.A. in communication, a B.S. in diplomacy in the workplace, an M.A.

in child development, a Ph.D. in the wisdom of experience . . . Take a moment now to write down your degrees.

Then, close your eyes and focus on your breathing for a minute or two. If your mind wanders, gently bring it back to concentrating on your breath. Imagine yourself at the prestigious University of Life impressively gowned and hooded. See a smiling, wise, and loving mentor awarding you the degrees and honors you richly deserve. Receive them graciously, knowing you have earned them and are worthy of each.

*I give myself credit for what I know
and what I am learning.*

I value the wisdom I've gained through experience.

Dethroning the Virgin

WHEN GROWING UP, MANY WOMEN WERE led to believe the only part of them that was acceptable to nice boys was the virgin. Pure, devoted, perfect, an object of respect and worship—a girl he'd be proud to take home to Mother. Of course bad boys seemed to want something else. How confusing for us if we were heart-thumpingly attracted to the bad boys we were afraid for our mothers to meet. If we were attracted to, or repulsed by, bad boys it was probably because they represented shadowy parts of ourselves that, on our pure pinnacle of pseudo-perfectionism, we were busily disowning—the rebel, harlot, and playful parts in us we felt were unacceptable.

Even as adults we often still carry the belief that, in order to be acceptable, we have to epitomize the ideal of virgin perfection. But we need to begin to understand we aren't, can't, and probably don't even want to be only the virgin. Rather, we can take the good parts of the virgin ideal—such as gentleness and purity of thought—and leave perfectionism behind.

For all of us, dethroning the virgin does not mean banishing her from the palace altogether. It means realizing the virgin in ourselves is a realistic and healthy part of our being—not the whole shebang. As long as the virgin is our only acceptable way of being, or even a large percentage, we set ourselves up to feel ashamed of our imperfections, our very humanness. And shame, in all of its various disguises, does need to be kicked out of the throne room. We do not need to be perfect to be acceptable to ourselves or others.

I have the courage to revel in my humanness.

*I accept all of my different selves
into the throne room of my heart.*

I am perfectly acceptable just the way I am.

Tapping Invisible Power

....

ALTHOUGH WE MAY THINK OF IT BY different names—God, Spirit, or Guardian Angel, for example—there is an invisible source of power around and within us waiting for us to call on it when we need it. Too often we ignore this presence out of ignorance, doubt, or forgetfulness.

Annabelle is a person who remembers and uses her power. One dark night the power came to her aid in a dramatic fashion. She was settling down for her first night at a retreat center in the California foothills when she realized she needed something from her car. Carefully making her way, she stepped back into what appeared to be tall grass at the edge of the parking lot. Seconds later she woke up in a six-foot culvert. Wedged in head first, she could not right herself or climb out. Feeling blood on the back of her head, she thought, "No one knows I'm here, and it's midnight." Instead of panicking, she said, "Father, I need your help." Suddenly, with no memory of how it happened, she found herself standing beside her car!

To help you connect with the presence

within and around you, close your eyes and allow yourself to move deeply into the center of your being, a place within you that is filled with gratitude for the mysteries of life. As you inhale say, "For your power," and as you exhale say, "I thank you." Gently continue this breath prayer for a few minutes, allowing a sense of peace to fill your heart.

We all possess incredible power. We are invited to have the courage to own it, use it wisely, and be thankful for it.

I tap into the invisible power in and around me.

I am surrounded by forces that love and protect me.

I thankfully accept the love and wisdom of my Goddess within.

Making a Difference

MOTHER TERESA HAS A SAYING THAT exemplifies Goddess energy: "Do small things with great love." My husband expanded this to say, "Doing small things with great love makes a big difference!" All of our lives are filled with literally millions of opportunities to do small things and make a big difference.

One day in Hawaii a ferocious storm washed hundreds of starfish ashore. A woman, on her morning walk, bent down every few steps to throw a starfish back into the sea. A man saw her and commented, "There are so many of the poor things it can't make any real difference for you to throw these few back." With a knowing smile, she tossed another starfish into the water and turning to the man said, "It made a difference to that one."

We can all make a difference. Often we don't even know when we have touched someone's life in a positive manner—a Goddess way. By ministering out of our ordinary experiences—expressing truthfully who we are—we create extraordinary differences in other lives. We all possess the Goddess energy, and when we illuminate a fragment of our own being through understanding and awareness, we naturally light the road for others.

I make a difference.

I do small things with great love.

*I express my Goddess energy
by being truly who I am.*

Assimilating Both
Saber and Scepter

REMEMBER THE CHILD'S RHYME, "WHAT are little girls made of? Sugar and spice and everything nice. What are little boys made of? Frogs and snails and puppy dog tails." As a little girl I used to think, "What a drag. I'd much rather be a boy."

This seemingly harmless little ditty exemplifies what so many of us were taught—that we must be nice and sweet. Hidden in the message was the belief that power and authority were not sweet and nice and thereby were only masculine prerogatives. Both the saber of power and the scepter of authority, or at least an outward show of them, were deemed somehow contradictory to our femininity.

This of course is not so. It takes a lot of strength and power to have a baby, speak our feelings, be intimate, make a living, be a peacemaker, and juggle the many details of everyday life. We women are now beginning to reclaim, outwardly, what we have suspected all along but were afraid to acknowledge—we are strong; we do have power and authority.

Our job now is to have the courage to assimilate the saber of power and the scepter of authority into our lives in a gentle, loving, and feminine way—from an essence of love and a desire for the empowerment of all people, not just a select, safe few. The first step in this process is to love and accept ourselves—our strengths and weaknesses, our power and vulnerabilities. We are each called to take up the saber and the scepter in our own lives.

I am powerful and strong.

I love being a woman.

*I use my power and authority
gently and with love.*

Serving as a Vessel

....

A PRIESTESS IS ONE WHO ACTS AS A channel for The Divine—a clear, strong vessel able to hold and disperse spiritual energy. She helps others by sharing what she has learned from the painful struggles in her own life. Using that definition, aren't we all in training to be a priestess?

In order to be a strong and useful vessel we must first endure the potter's fire. Annie, a beautiful and educated woman, works with a hospice bereavement program. People feel safe expressing even their darkest feelings in her presence. She doesn't have to say much; an aura of understanding and acceptance flows from her toward those who are grieving. Why? Because she has been through her personal fire—the death of one of her children—and emerged a stronger and more empathetic vessel for divine energy.

Pain can be an incubator for compassion, as it was for Annie, if we keep our intention toward healing, learning, and serving. When we view our pain as an instrument of growth and an opportunity to, eventually, be better able to serve others, it takes on a greater meaning. As we know, it is easier to endure that which has meaning for us than that which seems totally senseless. Being courageous enough to see painful circumstances in our lives as occasions to perfect the vessel we are allows us to take the meaning of our lives to its highest point.

I reach out to others in empathy and understanding.

I have the courage to find meaning in even my deepest pain.

I see myself as a vessel for divine energy and find joy in serving others.

Transforming and
Transmuting Circumstances

....

WHEN MY YOUNGEST SON WAS NINE years old, he and I were riding our bikes along the shoulder of Kalanianiole Highway in Honolulu. Contentedly following my son, I suddenly "saw" in my mind's eye a pickup truck swerve and hit him. I then "saw" myself in the middle of the street holding him while begging someone to call an ambulance. Remembering a formula I'd been taught for transforming and altering circumstances, I prayed, "Father/Mother God, I ask for the transformation and transmutation of what I just saw and for the perfect, right happening to occur instead." At that moment, a red pickup truck swerved onto the shoulder, missing my son by only a few inches.

Often, when we pay close attention, our intuition will give us previews of coming attractions or detractions. Alerted to what may happen, we then have the opportunity to ask for a change in unwanted circumstances. Learning to trust our intuition is one of our most challenging lessons. But when we have the courage to listen to our inner voice and the strength to act on what we hear, we are connecting with the wisdom of the Goddess within

I pay attention to my intuition.

I have the courage to trust my intuition.

*I use my inner wisdom and power
to alter circumstances.*

Gleaning Wisdom from Silence

WISDOM BEGINS IN SILENCE. AMID THE clatter, clack, and cacophony of our usual daily existence, how can we expect to hear the whisper of our wisdom and intuition? Having the courage to discipline ourselves to make time for silence, a time in which we can pay attention, is a real challenge. But unless we do, we will be aware of only a fraction of our selves.

Abraham Kawai, a Hawaiian teacher/healer, says that although his students learn many things, his entire teaching could be summed up in two words—pay attention. Interestingly, the opposite of "attention" is to "disregard and neglect." How often do we disregard our still, small voice—the voice of the Goddess within? How often do we neglect being silent and, therefore, make it impossible to hear the quiet messages she whispers to us concerning what is best for us to do, say, or be?

Take a moment now to listen, to pay attention to your inner voice. Find a place where you will not be disturbed and sit upright in a comfortable position. If you have a question or a problem that needs answering, jot it down on a piece of paper and then keep the paper beside you as you move into this quiet time. Tune in to your breathing, concentrate only on your breath entering and exiting your body. If thoughts intrude, bless them and allow them to effortlessly float out of your mind. Return your attention to your breath.

Do this simple exercise for only as long as it is comfortable. The last minute or two say "I" as you inhale and "know" as you exhale. Very gently open your eyes and randomly write down any thoughts that present themselves to you. They may or may not appear to have any connection to your original question. It doesn't matter. As you become accustomed to letting ideas pour forth freely, you will glean wisdom from the silence.

I pay attention to the Goddess within.

I have all of my answers inside of myself.

Transcending the Trojan Horse

IN THE LEGENDARY TROJAN WAR THE patriarchal Greeks overcame the matriarchal Trojans by trickery. The huge Trojan horse, a supposed peace offering from the Greeks, which they said would make Troy impregnable, was invited inside the walls of Troy. As the Trojans slept, Greek troops hidden inside the horse opened the gates to their waiting army. Troy was burned, and the Greeks won the war.

As this parable illustrates, feminine energy has been "asleep" for centuries while masculine energy and values took over religion and politics and became revered as the only way. But we, as modern Trojan women, have awakened to the need for balance in all aspects of our lives and culture. Warlike masculine qualities of dominance, competition, and conquest, untempered by the spiritual and nurturing qualities of the feminine, have finally endangered the very Mother who sustains us—Planet Earth. We must honor, balance, and synthesize both masculine and feminine energy now, in the microcosm of ourselves and the macrocosm of our world.

Take a few moments to list the feminine and masculine qualities you would like to embody. Close your eyes and visualize someone or something that epitomizes the positive masculine qualities. He can be a real person whom you respect and admire or a symbol your wise subconscious presents to you. Invite him to be an honored and valued part of your inner entourage. Do the same visualization for the feminine qualities you wish to personify.

As we move through our days we need to be willing to incorporate both masculine and feminine energy and attributes within ourselves.

*I value both my feminine and
masculine qualities.*

*I create peace and harmony on our planet
by first creating peace and harmony
within myself.*

Adopting a Mentor-Mom

. . . .

WHEN FAMILIES STAYED IN THE SAME
town with farms and businesses passing from
generation to generation, women naturally
received love, wisdom, and caring from older
women; maybe a mother, grandmother, or
wise aunt became a source of inspiration and
comfort for a young woman. So often now,
however, we are far from family, cut off from
relatives by distance or estrangement. Yet the
need to glean wisdom from an older woman's
experience is very much with us. An older
woman can turn from her place on the path
ahead of us and shed light on where we are at
the moment. She has been there.

If we have the mistaken idea that, in order
to be adult and mature, we need to go it
alone, we should remember that even the
most successful and talented athletes have
coaches who guide, encourage, and instruct
them. We need coaches, too. It is important
that we learn from the example of others who
have successfully been down the road we are
traveling.

If we don't already have a mentor-mom, we
need to begin looking for an older woman

whom we admire and trust, a woman into whose lap we can crawl when the going gets tough, and at whose feet (symbolically speaking) we can receive wise guidance. As we grow in age, experience, and wisdom, we can continue the circle of mentoring and sisterhood by extending our hand to a younger woman.

Women have much to give each other. We strengthen our Goddess within when we adopt one or more mentor-moms and bless ourselves in the rays of their love.

I give myself the gift of adopting a mentor-mom.

I welcome_____into my life
as a source of comfort, inspiration, and wisdom.

Doing No Harm

IMAGINE WHAT THE WORLD WOULD BE like if no one harmed anything or anyone. Wars would cease, rain forests would flourish, babies would be free of bruises and broken bones, women would not be battling the effects of inequality, criticism, and rejection. How can such a dream become a reality? Beginning with ourselves, we can courageously and consciously adopt the gentle attitude of doing no harm. Before we speak or act, we can stop and ask ourselves, "Will what I am about to say or do harm this person or thing?"

We already, at some conscious or unconscious level, live out the desire to do no harm. We may gently pick up a spider and put it outdoors instead of killing it. Or we may thoughtfully alter a statement we're about to make if we know it may be hurtful. But we need to be sure to include ourselves in this accepting attitude of treating all people and things with respect.

An interesting thing happens as we begin to practice harmless living; an awareness of the sacredness of all existence, ourselves included, begins to dawn on us. We begin to sense the Goddess/God in everything. We begin to experience a reverence for life, both animate and inanimate, that, in turn, creates serenity in our hearts and minds.

By expanding our desire not to harm, we create a powerful pebble-in-the-pond phenomenon. The ever-widening circles of respect and love we create touch countless people.

I am respectful of everything and everyone.

I consciously practice harmless living.

I have reverence for all life.

Personal Note

If *The Woman's Book of Courage* feels like a helpful friend to you, then, both as a woman and a writer, I am very happy. As we find the courage to embark on the sometimes frightening path toward increased authenticity, we all need hands to hold. Through this book maybe we can, in effect, hold each others' hands. May your journey be filled with the laughter of your healed inner child, a rainbow of miracles, and close communion with your Goddess within.

If you have ideas or experiences you would like to share, or if you would like to purchase autographed copies of any of my books, please write to me:

Sue Patton Thoele
P.O. Box 1519
Boulder, CO 80306-1519

Sue Patton Thoele

Sue Patton Thoele was a psychotherapist for twenty years, but is now concentrating on her passion for writing. She and her husband, Gene, live in Boulder, Colorado, and have four adult children and one grandchild.